BY **STEVE PEREZ** with Adam Kay

mi casa

Spanish-inspired recipes from the heart of Derbyshire

mi **casa**

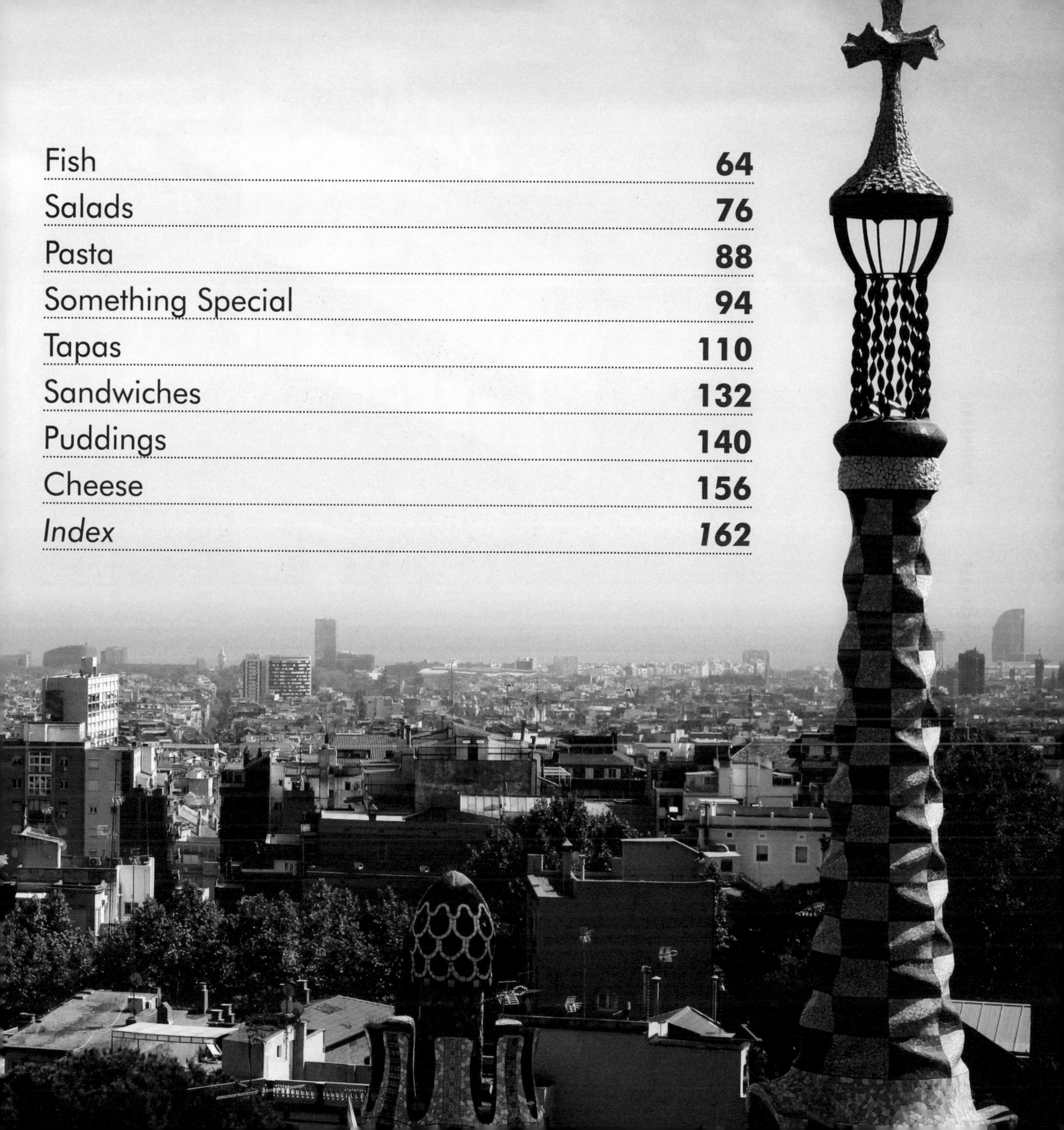

Welcome to Casa

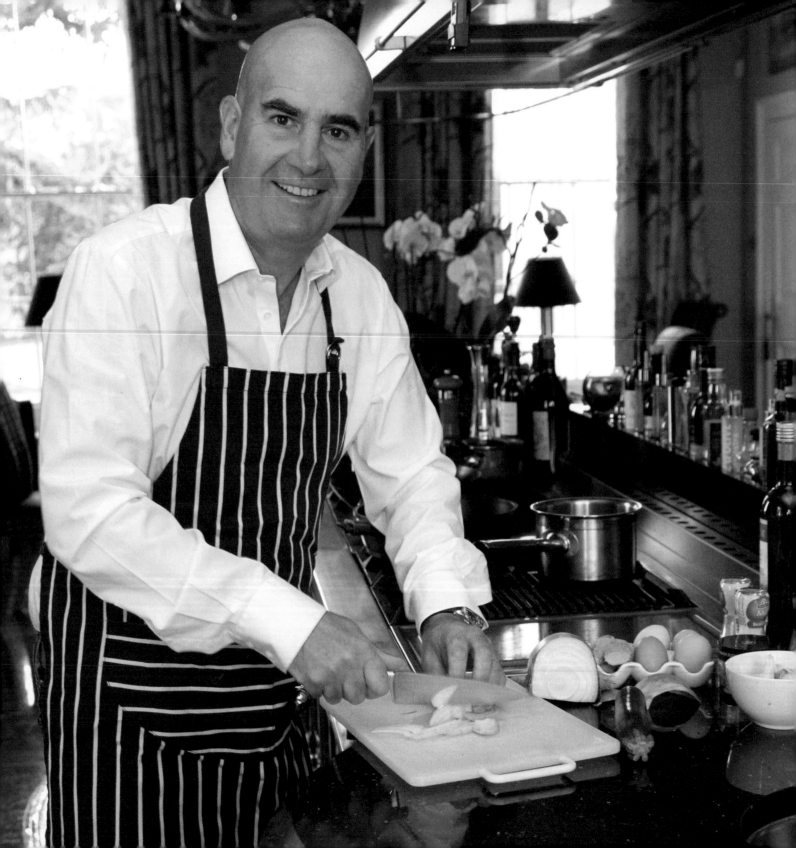

Steve Perez
Owner

It's amazing how the smallest things can trigger the most special memories. For me, the best example of this is food.

The taste of acorn-fed ibérico ham reminds me of being in a noisy bar in Las Ramblas, straining to hear over the excited chatter of the locals. The smell of fresh fish and garlic prawns brings to mind a beach restaurant in Mallorca, the clear Mediterranean skies overhead, the warmth of the Spanish sun on my face.

When it came to opening a hotel, I wanted to create somewhere which would be similarly evocative. Taking inspiration from my own Spanish heritage, I wanted it to offer people a taste of Spain – not just with food, but with every aspect of the hotel.

More importantly, I wanted it to be a place where people would make special memories of their own – spend happy times with loved ones and friends old and new. The name 'Casa', of course, means 'home' in Spanish, and that's exactly what I wanted the hotel to feel like – home.

Hopefully it does. And hopefully the memories – and recipes – shared in this book will make it a welcome addition to your own 'casa' too.

It can sometimes be a little bit hard to explain exactly what we do at Casa, but I'll give it a go. We're the only four-star hotel in Chesterfield, a historic market town in the north of England. We're passionate about food, and in particular local produce. And as the hotel is my baby, as it were, it reflects lots of different facets of my own personality – my Spanish background being just one of them.

As the founder of Global Brands, the UK's leading drinks brand development company, I'm a successful businessman. I'm also the current British Rally Champion, with four British titles under my belt. But in the back of my mind I'd always had a yearning to have a hotel or restaurant. And that stems from a love for food which began when I was very young.

My father, Santiago Garcia Perez, was a restaurateur in Derbyshire. Originally from Barcelona, he was one of the first people to bring Mediterranean food to the area back in the 1960s.

The place he and our family ran was the Red Lion at Stonedge. It's more of a pub now, but then it was very much a restaurant, and a busy and successful one at that. We had traditional tapas on the menu, and things like pepito, which is a Spanish steak sandwich, and of course paella.

Being surrounded by Spanish food had a huge influence on me. Despite the fact that I was brought up in Chesterfield, one of the UK's most distant towns from the coast, we ate a lot of fish at home. I still enjoy seafood now – one of my favourite fish is turbot, and I love sea bass, which we have on the menu at Casa. We often had calamari at home, and *pan con tomate* – bread with tomatoes and garlic. That's one of the things I remember eating as a boy and really enjoying.

It was perhaps inevitable that I'd end up following in my father's footsteps, and sure enough my first career was in the restaurant business. I spent time working in Barcelona as a waiter, and also as a chef. I then did the same back in England, then developed my career and worked my way up to managing pubs.

I soon got fed up of working for the big corporate companies, so I started what was basically a 'man-and-a-van' business, delivering imported beers to local pubs. The business grew and grew, and during that time I noticed that the ready-to-drink market was doing very well.

In a flash of inspiration, I came up with a drink of my own, VK (Vodka Kick), which became a huge success.

In 2002 I was CBI's Entrepreneur of the Year, and in 2003 my company – later renamed Global Brands Ltd – was named the UK's third fastest-growing business by the Sunday Times.

The business continued to go from strength to strength, but there was one downside to being based in Chesterfield: the lack of good hospitality venues. When I needed to entertain customers, I struggled to find places to take them out for food, or suitable overnight accommodation.

To me, it made logical sense to open a hotel of my own in the area – and in 2010, that's exactly what I did.

As a businessman, I've travelled the world and stayed in lots of different hotels, so I know what separates the good ones from the bad. Often, the food on offer is the make-or-break factor: an awful meal can spoil your whole impression of the hotel, whereas a fantastic one can make your experience truly special.

With my restaurant background, I knew I wanted the focus at Casa to be on food. Not necessarily formal fine dining – just great local ingredients, cooked with skill and a little Mediterranean flair. Cocina (Spanish for 'kitchen') is Casa's in-house restaurant. Food is also served in the Barça Bar, the hotel's stylish lounge. In both, you'll find delicious dishes all freshly prepared by head chef Andy Wilson and his talented team.

The ingredients are of particular importance. One of my life's passions is farming, and most of the meat and eggs used at Casa come from my own 350-acre Walton Lodge Farm, less than five miles up the road from the hotel.

A lot of the dishes on Casa's menus are also really healthy. My other passion in life is rally driving, and as a result I work out a lot and take care over my personal fitness and health. I wanted our guests to be able to dine here every night of their stay if they wanted to, without being faced with only heavy meals like steak and chips every night.

Indeed, having a wide range of dining options is central to the whole ethos of Casa. Usually hotel restaurants are either Michelin-starred, serving fancy meals made with rich ingredients, or bland and uninspiring. At Casa, you can celebrate a special occasion with an elegant plate of food, or enjoy something just as tasty but simpler, more relaxed. We cater for classy and casual equally well.

I'm heavily involved in every aspect of the food served at Casa – from providing the hotel with produce from my own farm, to tasting every single dish that goes on the menus. I even help to pick (and test) the wine list – one of the perks of the job…

The offices of my drinks company, Global Brands Ltd, are based at Casa now, so I do tend to eat here quite a lot out of necessity. But I eat here out of choice as well – and that's because I truly believe we serve some of the best food in the country.

I consider myself very fortunate to have Spanish roots. Such a beautiful country, such wonderful people and, of course, such incredible food.

I'm still as passionate about food as I ever was. I can spend as much time talking about the making of a good sandwich as I can about doing a deal with a big supermarket group!

It's particularly important to me that Casa offers an authentic Spanish eating experience, or as much of one as possible. Hopefully this will introduce as many people as possible to the Spanish cuisine I love so much. One taste, and I'm certain they'll love it too.

I have a house in Andratx, Mallorca, and I spend quite a lot of time there. Whenever I'm in Spain, I eat out regularly and try a lot of different restaurants. I always speak to the chefs, and get recipes and ideas to bring back to Casa.

My phone is full of photographs of the food I eat on my travels. Often, I'll send these pictures to Andy and the chefs at Casa: "Look at this great sandwich! Why don't we try something like this? That's how a salad should look!"

I'm constantly looking for new ideas and ways of improving what we do. The team know I used to be a chef, so they appreciate my comments, and we work together to replicate the fabulous dishes and flavours of Spain. The Josper oven is a classic example of something I spotted while I was abroad and knew I wanted to introduce back at the hotel. It's a charcoal oven which combines the cooking performance of a regular oven with the great flavour of a grill. I watched a guy cooking on one in Barcelona and thought they would work great at Casa, and sure enough they've proved to be a huge hit.

17

The Josper helps us to recreate those authentic Spanish flavours, but we also try to source real Spanish ingredients wherever we can. Because I spend so much time over in Spain, I can tell when a piece of ham or cheese is a poor imitation – not jamón serrano or manchego. To get hold of the real deal, we work with fantastic suppliers such as Grey's Fine Foods.

The dishes on our menus have to be authentic as well. Things like tapas are prepared according to the recipes I learned as a child or young chef, or ones I've subsequently picked up during time spent in Spain. We don't claim to offer a definitive Spanish dining experience, because in fact there's no such thing. The country's cuisine is incredibly diverse, with many regional variations – if you go into a restaurant in Spain, it's not necessarily just paella every night.

Our menus are based on my own favourite bits of Spanish gastronomy – dishes I've discovered which I want our guests to enjoy as well. And while it may not be traditional in every region of Spain, we do serve a great paella – it's one of my favourite things to cook at home.

The food we serve isn't exclusively Spanish or Mediterranean, either. You'll also find poached salmon on the menu, for example, simple scallops, a great steak or burger.

What we're trying to do at Casa is give people a taste of Spain. The only thing we can't provide is the sunshine…

The Spanish influence doesn't only extend to the food, though. The suites here are all named after famous Spanish artists – Dalí, Picasso, and so on. Obviously this fits in with the theme of the hotel, and it also stems from my own interest in art.

I often bring back bits of artwork from abroad. There are prints of paintings by Miró and many others adorning the walls of the hotel. As for the statue on reception, I saw him on my travels and thought he'd be perfect for the hotel, so there he stands. It's by an artist called Bruno Catalano, and is titled 'J'Attends' – I am waiting.

If you go into the Cocina Restaurant, you'll find some of my family photographs all around the walls – pictures of me when I was a kid, my father and uncle working in restaurants and so on. That thread of my history runs throughout the hotel, and it's one of the things that makes it unique.

Casa is the result of a lot of blood, sweat and tears – not just my own, but all the people involved in helping to build and create the hotel. So it feels very special when our labour of love is showered with praise and accolades.

The Cocina Restaurant has two prestigious AA rosettes, something we're extremely proud of. Casa itself is listed as one of the UK's top 10 hotels by the website TripAdvisor. We've won a host of other national and local awards too, and each and every one of them makes us feel like our efforts have been worthwhile.

But while all these plaudits are amazing, winning awards isn't our main focus. The most important thing is giving our guests a great experience. At Casa, we've got a brilliant team dedicated to doing just that.

Head chef Andy Wilson has been with us from the very beginning. He brought with him some serious culinary

pedigree: a background in Michelin-starred restaurants and top hotels, including a stint at the legendary Claridge's. Andy started at Casa as sous chef, before being put in charge of the kitchen in 2011. Since then, he's stamped his own personality on the dishes, while staying true to the ethos of the hotel.

Andy's passion for food and constant quest for perfection is a real inspiration. With him at the helm, Casa's kitchen team continue to produce the stunning dishes we've become renowned for.

This enthusiasm isn't just confined to the kitchen, however – it's something which the entire Casa team shares. In everything we do here, we all strive to improve – to make the hotel as good as it can possibly be.

I believe that if you offer people a great experience, they'll come back for more. Judging by the number of satisfied customers who've made regular return visits to Casa, I think we must be doing something right.

So why a Casa cookbook, then?

Firstly, it's a memento for our guests – a present they can take home as a reminder of a memorable stay.

But it's also a way of explaining a bit more about what we do here, and why we do it. When it comes to food, we have a very particular approach.

I'm a firm believer in the merits of buying local. It's better from an economic point of view, with money spent being pumped back into the local area, and also from an environmental one, by reducing 'food miles' – the distance ingredients travel from field to fork. Most of all, however, food and ingredients bought locally are invariably better quality than those bought elsewhere. They simply taste better.

Throughout the book, you'll also find information about some of the great local suppliers we use at Casa. Much more than just business partners, these fabulous foodies have become trusted friends of the hotel, and it's a joy to be able to use their fantastic produce in our cooking.

We're blessed with some wonderful food producers here in Derbyshire. But wherever you are in the country, you'll find people with a similar love of food and a commitment to quality. I implore you to avoid the big supermarkets whenever you can, and seek out your local butcher, greengrocer and fish merchant instead. Your tastebuds will thank you for it.

Food doesn't have to be complicated – I'm a big believer in that. A lot of the dishes in this book are quite simple to make, but that doesn't mean they're any less delicious. The key is to get the best, freshest ingredients you possibly can – and here's another tip: don't lose all of the freshness and flavour from those ingredients by overcooking them. Less is more.

You'll find a varied range of dishes throughout the book, and I hope you enjoy cooking them all. Even if you don't follow the recipes line for line, you might pick up a few ideas.

Hopefully when you cook these dishes for yourself, you'll be transported to that bar in Las Ramblas, to the beach restaurant in Mallorca with the sun beating down hot on your face.

A taste of Spain in your very own home: what could be more memorable than that?

Store
Cupboard
Essentials

* Onions/shallots
* Garlic
* Rosemary
* Thyme
* Parsley
* Lemons
* Shop-bought beef and/or chicken stock (or stock cubes will suffice in most cases)
* Saffron

* Salt (table and Maldon salt)
* Black peppercorns
* Ground white pepper
* Tinned chopped tomatoes
* Tomato purée
* Vanilla pods (not essence)
* Caster sugar
* Free range eggs
* Arrowroot (for thickening sauces)

* Tinned beans/chickpeas, etc
* Dried herbs and spices
* White wine vinegar
* Sherry vinegar
* Red and white wine for cooking (decent quality; if it doesn't taste nice in the bottle, it won't taste nice in your cooking)
* Port
* Madeira

* Anchovies
* Manchego cheese
* Chorizo
* Jamón ibérico
* Smoked paprika
* Capers
* Olives
* Pimientos

Fine food should be complemented with great drinks. With that in mind, here are our recommendations, courtesy of Casa's sister company, Global Brands Ltd.

Amigos

An easy-drinking tequila-flavoured beer with a hint of South American limes, Amigos is a zesty and refreshing beverage, filled with Aztec spirit.

True to the South American influence which inspired it, it's a perfect match for spicy dishes such as **gambas pil pil** or **penne pasta with chorizo and smoked bacon in a spicy tomato sauce**. Its hints of citrus cut through intense and hot flavours to keep the palate refreshed.

Hooper's

Hooper's is a range of traditionally British alcoholic brews, made using natural fruit flavours and real fruit juices. The drinks have been designed to partner well with food, and each flavour has its own distinct qualities.

The dark fruity tones of Hooper's Dandelion & Burdock make it an ideal match for hearty dishes such as **roast duck with a celeriac puree, grilled asparagus, roasted new potatoes and a red wine and cherry jus**; the sweet berry notes of Hooper's Raspberry & Nettle are a brilliant accompaniment to dessert; while the wonderful zestiness of Hooper's Cloudy Lemonade partners well with rich flavours, such as **oven roast chicken supreme with mashed potato, truffled baby leeks, pancetta bacon and baby gem**.

Thorntons Chocolate Liqueur

Guaranteed to delight chocolate lovers, Thorntons Chocolate Liqueur combines the superior taste of West African cocoa with cream and smooth vodka for a luxuriously rich after-dinner indulgence. The perfect way to round off your delicious meal.

The Perez Paella

Serves 6

INGREDIENTS

For the paella stock:

A dash of rapeseed oil, for cooking

1 medium-sized bulb of fennel

1 diced white onion

4 cloves chopped garlic

1kg crab bodies/prawn shells

1 star anise

A pinch of saffron

300ml dry white wine

1.5l fish stock (shop-bought will be fine)

100g tomato purée

500ml water (optional – use to top up the stock if needed)

Salt and pepper, to season

METHOD

In a pan big enough to take the crab bodies/prawn shells, add a dash of oil and sweat off the fennel, onion and garlic with no colour. Add in the crab bodies/prawn shells and turn up the heat to roast the shells for flavour.

When the shells have roasted slightly – after 2-5 minutes – turn down the heat, add the tomato purée and cook this for 10 minutes.

Add the star anise, saffron and white wine. Reduce the wine until it has nearly all evaporated to remove any bitterness from the alcohol, then add the fish stock and top up with water to cover all the shells so they are submerged in the liquid.

Simmer for 30 minutes and taste. Season lightly at this stage (don't over-season, as when you cook your paella this stock will reduce in the cooking process and potentially leave you with salty paella).

If you have a good quality blender and you've used prawn shells then blend well and pass through a sieve, squeezing with the back of a ladle to ensure you get as much yield as possible. If you have used crab bodies, remove them first and let the liquid strain from the shells into a bowl under a colander – the crab shells would most likely break your blender. Pass the liquid either through a piece of muslin cloth or a clean tea towel to remove any shell particles and so forth.

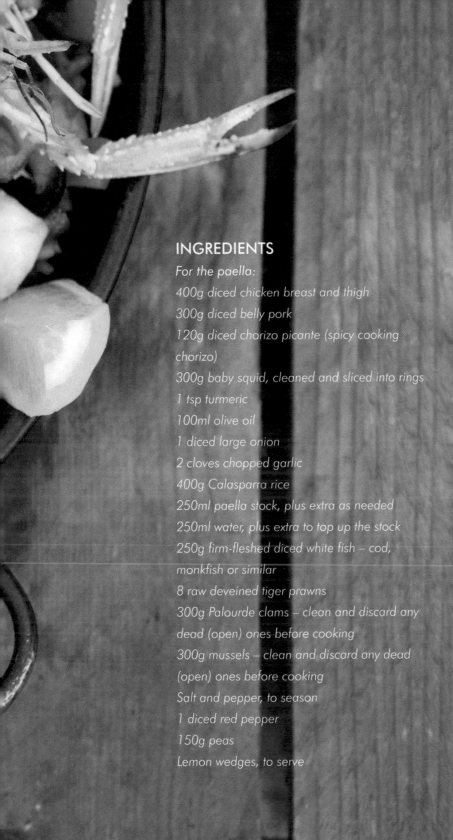

INGREDIENTS

For the paella:
400g diced chicken breast and thigh
300g diced belly pork
120g diced chorizo picante (spicy cooking chorizo)
300g baby squid, cleaned and sliced into rings
1 tsp turmeric
100ml olive oil
1 diced large onion
2 cloves chopped garlic
400g Calasparra rice
250ml paella stock, plus extra as needed
250ml water, plus extra to top up the stock
250g firm-fleshed diced white fish – cod, monkfish or similar
8 raw deveined tiger prawns
300g Palourde clams – clean and discard any dead (open) ones before cooking
300g mussels – clean and discard any dead (open) ones before cooking
Salt and pepper, to season
1 diced red pepper
150g peas
Lemon wedges, to serve

METHOD

In a hot paella dish, fry off and brown the chicken, belly pork, chorizo, squid and turmeric in the olive oil. Add the diced onion and garlic, reduce the heat and cook until opaque, then add the rice and cook in the oils for 2 minutes to allow every grain to be coated. This will prevent the rice from clumping together.

Add 250ml of your paella stock and 250ml of water and turn down to a simmer. Add more stock or water during the cooking process to allow the rice to cook through until tender.

After roughly 10 minutes, taste a piece of rice. If it has started to soften, adjust the seasoning then arrange your diced white fish, prawns, clams and mussels in an attractive manner on the rice.

Sauté your diced red pepper and cook your peas, and scatter onto the paella.

When the rice is tender – after about 20 minutes – remove from the heat and allow to stand somewhere warm for 5-10 minutes. This will allow the rice to absorb any remaining stock. Serve with wedges of lemon and enjoy.

The Josper oven is a Spanish-designed charcoal-fuelled oven from Barcelona. They are becoming more commonplace in kitchens around the country now, but when Casa first opened there were only a handful of other establishments in the UK that were using them.

We are lucky enough to have two Jospers at Casa. One is used to produce food for the Barça Bar, and also for barbecues for weddings and so on. We take this oven out onto the terrace and cook the food in front of the guests for their wedding or event. The other larger Josper is situated at the front of the Cocina Restaurant, which has an open kitchen so that guests can see the Josper in action and literally watch their food being cooked if they so desire.

We mainly use the Josper in Cocina for the three types of steak that we serve, which are fillet, ribeye and sirloin. They are sourced from either Walton Lodge Farm or from other local farms, and all are hung for a minimum of 28 days.

The great thing about Josper ovens is the flavour that they give to meat and fish. They are marketed as an indoor barbecue and that's exactly how they work. Unlike a normal barbecue, however, we use ours at around 350-400 degrees centigrade, so even a rare steak will still have a lovely caramelised and smoky flavour that is normally very hard to achieve. We also cook fish on the bone and some of the tapas dishes through the Jospers. Even the pizza bases that we serve in the Barça Bar are first of all baked through these ovens, to give the pizza the slight smokiness you'd achieve using a wood-fired pizza oven.

Walton

Lodge Estate

We are all, to some degree, a product of our environment. My Spanish heritage influenced my choice of career as a chef, and years later has influenced Casa and the theme of the hotel.

But my Derbyshire upbringing has also played a big part in my life, inspiring one of my great passions: farming. And I'm now able to use that passion to benefit the hotel, through my own Walton Lodge Farm. Sometimes, it's funny how things come together.

My father's restaurant was out in the countryside, so I grew up with green fields around me. As a result, I'd always been fascinated by the fact that we get our food from the land – not only the fruits and vegetables that grow there, but also the animals that feed from it.

This sparked an interest in farming. When I started to get my first taste of business success, I bought a smallholding, on which I had a few head of cattle and grew my own vegetables. I took great pleasure from being able to go into my own garden and pick out vegetables that I'd grown to cook for family mealtimes.

Later, I moved into Walton Lodge and also bought the farm which was next door. I developed an interest – some would call it an obsession – in producing really good quality meat, initially for my own consumption. When the hotel came along, it provided an outlet for that fabulous meat, and an opportunity for me to share the fruits of my obsession with others.

Over the years, the Walton Lodge Estate has grown and grown. I've been lucky enough to acquire some of the land around the original site, taking the estate to its current 350 acres. The various fields have been tended to and fenced – there was no fencing at all when I first took over – and it's now a thriving business in its own right.

I'm still heavily involved in the operation of the farm – obviously I live on the estate, so whenever I'm not away on business, I check in every day to see how things are going. But these days, I leave the day-to-day running of Walton Lodge Farm in the capable hands of farm manager John Brailsford.

John has farming in his blood, and a close personal link with Walton Lodge too, as his grandfather farmed here years ago. His years of experience are an enormous asset to the business and, just as importantly, he's one of the nicest chaps you'll ever meet. He and I have been friends for a number of years, and when I needed someone to help out on the farm, I asked John, at first on a part-time basis. For the past seven years, he's worked here full-time, living with his wife in the farm cottage.

John lives and breathes farming – for him, it's not just a job but a passion. In his spare time, he's a judge at the British National Ploughing Championships, mentoring the next generation of farming talent.

John's input has been vital in getting Walton Lodge Farm to where it is today. We are fully Farm Assured and Red Tractor certified, and we don't intensively farm, but rather look after our animals. As a result, our produce is – we believe – the very finest in the area.

46

Our main commodity is cattle. We have long-haired Highlands and Belted Galloways, named for the 'belt' of white they have around their middle. With their round, fluffy ears, it's easy to become attached to them – they're almost like family. John's a typical down-to-earth farmer, but I know he always feels sad when he has to take an animal to the abattoir.

Our other livestock includes Dorset sheep and Gloucester Old Spot pigs, as well as free range Warren Hybrid hens – or "egg machines," as John jokingly calls them. And let's not forget the vegetables and fruit grown here, juicy apples and plums among them.

Walton Lodge Farm is a fantastic business to be involved with. We do have to make a profit, of course, but we're in the advantageous position of being able to take a bit more time and care over our operation than other farms. We can afford to keep things looking neat and tidy.

That's so much the better, because one of the best things about the Walton Lodge Estate is its wonderful grounds. Derbyshire is generally very pretty, but our small corner of it is especially beautiful. It's our intention to keep it that way.

We've planted hundreds of trees during our time here. We may not be able to enjoy them in our lifetimes, but it gives us real pleasure to know that future generations will.

John and I feel very humbled to have been able to play a part in the history of the Walton Lodge Estate and Farm. When you have somewhere as special as this to look after, work doesn't really feel like work.

Meat

We're big on meat here at Casa. We cater for vegetarians and vegans too, of course, but meat is definitely the star of the show.

That's in keeping with the Spanish theme of the hotel. Meat is central to the Spanish diet – particularly pork, and pork products like ham and cured sausage.

Almost all of the meat we use at the hotel comes from Walton Lodge Farm, but we also work with another fantastic local business: Highfield House Farm.

Based just up the road from both Casa and the Walton Lodge Estate, Highfield is a 110-acre farm owned and run by Dave Prince and his family. Dave is a master butcher, and that's not just empty praise – he has both the qualifications and the years of experience to prove it.

Because I live nearby, I've used Highfield as my local butcher for many years. When Casa was being built, Dave expressed an interest in working with us – whenever I used to pop in, he'd joke:

"We're still looking at your order, you know!" I thought about it, and really it was an easy decision to say yes – I knew we'd make a great partnership.

Our animals are killed humanely at a local slaughterhouse, before being sent to Highfield for butchery. Dave and his team hang the carcasses for about four weeks – our rare breeds take a little bit longer to mature than some others.

The carcasses are then split up into 'primals' – basically, broken down according to muscle groups. These are then vacuum-packed or wrapped in clingfilm, and sent over to Casa, where our kitchen team can prepare or portion them up ready to cook for our guests.

Fresh Fish Thursdays

SECOND PRIZE

FIRST PRIZE

SECOND PRIZE

British Pork Tenderloin
£12.00/kg
£5.44/lb

British Pork Loin Chops
£8.74/kg
£3.95/lb

British Fillet Steak
£43.65/kg

Farm Shop & Tea Rooms
HIGHFIELD HOUSE

FARM SHOP
→

MON - SAT 8AM - 5PM
SUN 9AM - 4PM

If we're ever short on particular cuts of meat for any reason, we'll buy it from Highfield; and similarly they take surplus from us when we have any. Dave always says Highfield are "big enough to cope and small enough to care." His passion for good customer service is almost as big as his expertise in butchery.

Indeed, that expertise is ingrained, and comes from a lifetime in the industry. Dave followed in the footsteps of his father, a butcher, working first in slaughterhouses before moving into the wholesale side of the business, with much success.

Dave's personal dream was to own a hobby farm before he was 40. In 1986 – aged 39 – he got one, when he and his family moved into Highfield.

When new European Economic Community rules affecting the industry came into force in 1993, Dave decided to focus on Highfield House Farm full-time. Three years later, it opened as a commercial business, with Dave's flocks of pedigree sheep the prime commodity.

Nowadays, business is booming. As well as working with Casa, Highfield supply nearby landmarks Brampton Manor and East Lodge, amongst others. Also, the onsite farm shop was expanded in 2014 and now includes a charming tea room, attracting visitors from far and wide.

At Highfield, Dave has assembled a team of expert butchers – he estimates there are over 200 years of experience between him and his employees. That's why we're so proud to work with Highfield – and why we're sure that we offer our guests at Casa the very best meat.

Read more about Highfield House Farm at www.highfieldhousefarm.co.uk.

Casa burger

This is the burger patty that we serve in the Barça bar at Casa – a very simple recipe. You could use normal lean minced beef as a cheaper alternative to minced rump tail, but if you do, don't serve the burgers pink in the middle – cook them through thoroughly instead.

INGREDIENTS

1kg minced rump tail

2 cloves crushed garlic

1 whole egg

20g salt and 20g freshly ground black pepper

4 burger buns

To serve (optional):

1 head romaine lettuce

4 sliced vine tomatoes

4 spoonfuls shop-bought tomato chutney

Aioli

A recommendation from John Hattersley Wines:

"A wine to match the flavours of the Casa burger, with all its spice and smoky flavours, must be the **Rioja Artesa Crianza**. Long juicy red wine flavours, very little oak and soft tannins will bring out the flavours in the meat."

METHOD

In a large bowl, add the mince, garlic, egg and seasoning and slowly work them together by squeezing the mince through your fingers until it has all combined. The key to getting a good end result is to mix everything by hand. If you do this in a mixer, the texture of the burger becomes rubbery and unpleasant.

Cook a little of the mix and taste so you can add more seasoning if necessary. Split the mix into four equal amounts. You can obviously weigh the mix out if you want it be exact, but this will give you roughly four 227g (8oz) burgers.

Work each portion of the mince into a tight ball using your hands. Lay out a piece of clingfilm and wrap each burger patty individually, pressing it into a burger shape as you do so. Allow the mix to firm up in the fridge for at least an hour, or the burgers will simply fall apart during cooking.

We cook our burgers on the Josper ovens, charcoal-fuelled Spanish ovens which create the same flavour as cooking on a barbecue. To replicate this I would recommend using a barbecue, or if the weather isn't suitable then simply pan-fry or grill the burgers to your own desired cooking degree.

We serve our burgers in a homemade bun with aioli (garlic mayonnaise), crisp romaine lettuce, sliced vine tomatoes and a homemade tomato chutney, but again decent quality shop-bought burger buns and sauces/chutneys will be fine as alternatives. The beef is obviously the main event in this dish.

Carpaccio of Walton Lodge beef fillet

Carpaccio of Walton Lodge beef fillet

Serves 4

The key to this dish is very good quality, well-aged beef. At the hotel we marinade a whole fillet and slice the beef paper-thin on a meat slicer, but the following way works just as well to make at home.

INGREDIENTS

4 x 57g (2oz) slices of beef fillet – we use Walton Lodge beef

Maldon salt, some for the marinade and some for the cream

Freshly milled black pepper, some for the marinade and some for the cream

Pinch of chopped lemon thyme

1 chopped mild red chilli

1 clove garlic, finely chopped

30g grated manchego or Parmesan cheese

100ml double cream

20g fresh horseradish, finely grated

Baby watercress, to dress

Chopped flat leaf parsley, to dress

Olive oil, to dress

You will also need:

Greaseproof paper

Meat mallet or rolling pin

METHOD

First of all, lay a piece of greaseproof paper on the worktop or a heavy wooden chopping board. Put one of the pieces of beef on top of the paper, put another piece of paper on top of the beef and then carefully but firmly with either a meat mallet or rolling pin hit the beef repeatedly, so as to make the beef as thin as possible without it tearing. When this is achieved, carefully remove the top layer of paper, get the plate you are going to serve the starter on and put the plate over the top of the thinly-sliced meat. Turn the plate over so that the paper is on the top, and carefully peel back the paper so the beef is left on the plate. Repeat this process with the other three pieces of beef, obviously using four separate plates.

Sprinkle the beef generously with the salt and freshly-milled black pepper, lemon thyme, chopped garlic, chopped chilli and cheese. Set aside at room temperature for about 20 minutes to allow the salt to partially cure the beef, and for the other flavours to be absorbed as well. Whip the cream to a firm peak and add horseradish to your own taste. Season with salt and pepper and put a quenelle (an egg shape achieved with two wet spoons) of the mixture in the middle of each piece of beef. Toss the watercress in olive oil, serve with the beef, dress with the chopped parsley, and that's it.

Oven roast chicken supreme

Serves 4

WITH MASHED POTATO, TRUFFLED BABY LEEKS, PANCETTA BACON & BABY GEM

....

INGREDIENTS

For the sauce:

Rapeseed oil, for cooking

2 shallots, peeled and roughly chopped

1 carrot, peeled and roughly chopped

1 stick celery, peeled and roughly chopped

1 bay leaf

2 cloves peeled and chopped garlic

1 sprig thyme

100ml medium dry white wine

1.14 litres (2 pints) brown chicken stock (available in supermarkets)

25g diced cold unsalted butter

For the chicken:

A splash of vegetable oil, for cooking

4 skin-on chicken breasts

200g diced pancetta/bacon

40 baby onions, peeled and cooked (frozen ones will do)

8 shiitake mushrooms, quartered

2 baby gem lettuces, washed and torn into bite-size pieces

Salt and pepper, to season

400g mashed potato (finished with double cream and butter to taste)

6 baby leeks, trimmed and cut into thin strips

10g chopped truffle (white truffle oil can be used instead)

Butter, for cooking

Continued on the next page...

Oven roast chicken supreme

METHOD

Start with the sauce: firstly, place a heavy-based saucepan over a medium to high heat. Add a splash of oil and add everything except the wine, chicken stock and butter. Roast the vegetables until they are nicely browned, but don't let them burn as this will make your sauce bitter. If they start to catch, add a splash of water to cool the pan down.

After about 5-10 minutes or when nicely coloured, add the white wine and reduce until the wine has nearly all evaporated. Add the stock and bring it to the boil, turn the heat down to a vigorous simmer and allow the stock to reduce until thickened to the consistency of single cream (roughly by two-thirds). Remove from the heat and pass through a fine sieve, pressing firmly so you get all the flavour from the vegetables.

Pre-heat the oven to 180 degrees centigrade, and in an ovenproof frying pan add a splash of oil. Season the chicken breasts and place them carefully into the pan skin side down. Allow the skin to achieve a light golden brown then turn the breasts over to seal the flesh side. After roughly a minute, return the chicken onto the skin side and place the pan into the oven. Cook the chicken for 12-18 minutes, turning occasionally to avoid burning the chicken. The breast should feel firm but with a little give, almost like a medium well-done steak. If unsure, check with a food probe and ensure the chicken has a core temperature of 70 degrees centigrade.

Remove from the oven and allow the meat to relax in the cooking dish. In a separate pan over a high heat, add your pancetta bacon and sauté until it starts to colour and crisp up slightly, then add your cooked baby onions and allow them to colour slightly. Next add the shiitake mushrooms and cook them until tender.

Add the chicken sauce that you made earlier and any juices from the pan with the cooked chicken breasts in it. Bring the sauce to the boil and whisk in the 25g of diced cold butter, as this will give the sauce a glossy finish and a rounded flavour. Check the seasoning, add the lettuce and take off the heat.

Reheat the mashed potato. In a new clean pan, add a little butter, add your leeks and chopped truffle (or truffle oil) and cook the leeks until tender – about 2 minutes. Split the sauce between 4 bowls. Into the centre of each bowl, add a quarter of the mashed potato and place the chicken on top of the mash. Finally, add the leeks to the top of the chicken breast and serve.

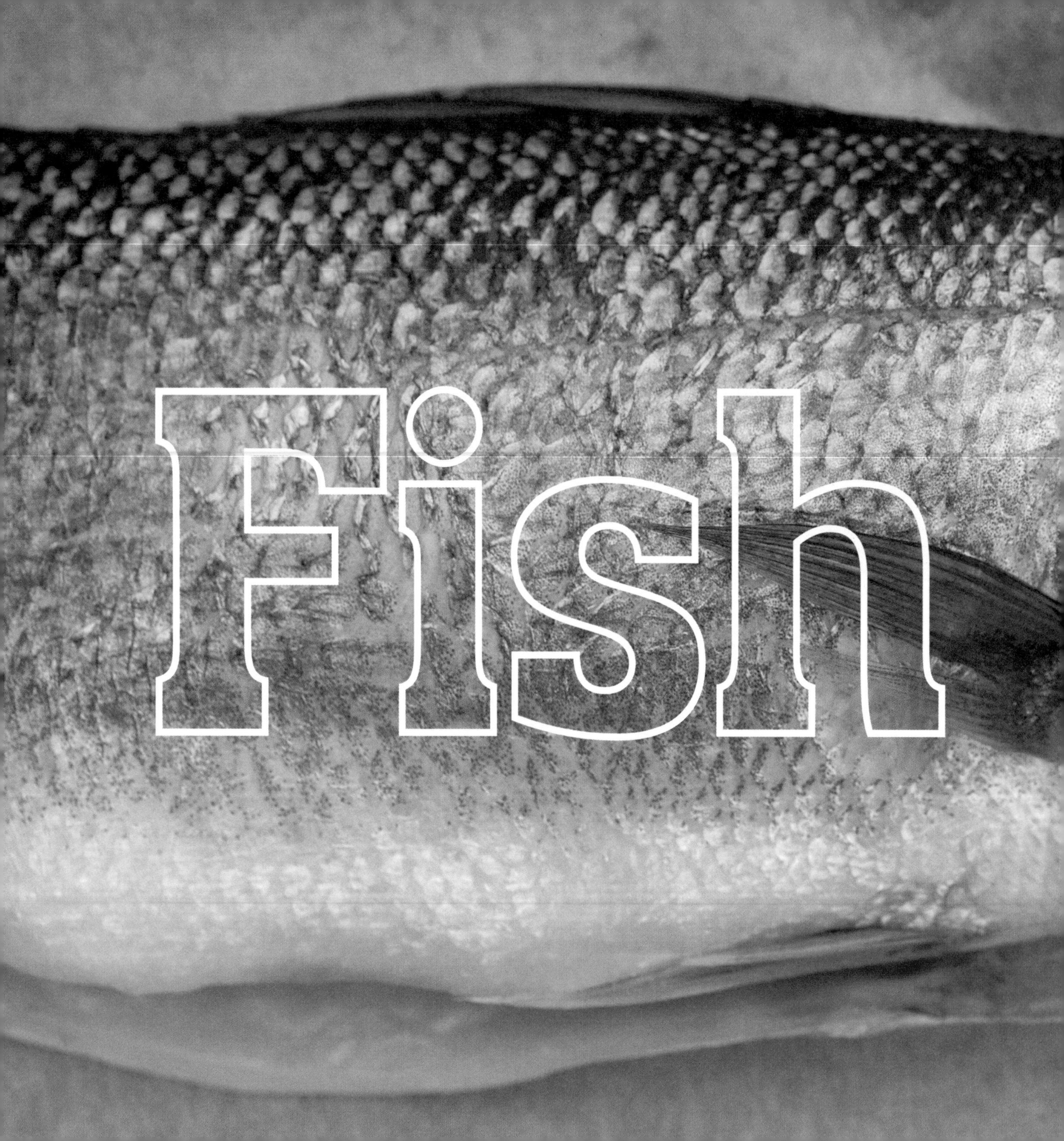
Fish

Roasted monkfish
WRAPPED IN SERRANO HAM WITH A CRAB, LEMON AND CHILLI RISOTTO

Roasted monkfish

INGREDIENTS

4 x 170-226g (6-8oz) portions of filleted monkfish tail

4 thin slices of serrano ham, big enough to wrap the fish

80ml olive oil, plus extra for cooking the fish

1 white Spanish onion, finely diced

1 banana shallot, finely diced

1 stick celery, finely diced

1 chopped medium hot chilli

1 bay leaf

1 sprig thyme, leaves removed

Salt and pepper, to season

1 litre vegetable or chicken stock

100g unsalted butter

500g Arborio rice

100ml double cream, plus an extra 100ml for the white wine and cream sauce (optional)

50g Parmesan, finely grated

Zest of 1 lemon, finely grated

150g cooked crab claw meat, preferably blue swimming crab

Chopped chives, to garnish

2 cloves garlic, finely chopped

200ml medium dry white wine

You will also need:

A non-stick ovenproof frying pan

A recommendation from John Hattersley Wines:

"With this dish, I would put the **Vetiver Rioja Blanco** from the mountains. The complexity and nasal notes of the wine will work well with the chilli risotto, complement the crab and stand up to the ham around the monkfish, and still let all the flavours of the food come through."

Serves 4

METHOD

Trim any sinew from your monkfish. Lay out a slice of the ham, place one of the portions of monkfish on top of it and roll the fish up in the ham, ensuring that it's nice and tight so that the ham doesn't unwrap whilst cooking. Repeat this with the other three pieces of fish, then place in the fridge for the fish to firm up.

Put your stock in a saucepan on a medium heat and bring it to the boil. Put a non-stick ovenproof frying pan over a medium heat, and also turn your oven to 180 degrees centigrade.

When the frying pan is hot, add a little oil, place your monkfish into it carefully and leave until the ham starts to turn a nice pink colour and crisp slightly. Turn the fish over and repeat this until you have the same result all around the fish. Place into the oven for roughly 8 minutes, turning once during cooking. Once cooked, remove and set aside.

Meanwhile, make the risotto. Place a saucepan over a medium heat, add the olive oil then the onion, shallot, garlic, celery, chilli, bay leaf and chopped thyme and season with salt and pepper. Sweat all these ingredients off together until the onions are opaque.

Add half the butter, and when it's melted put in the rice. Keep moving the rice around in the pan so that each grain of rice gets coated with the oil and butter, as this will stop the rice clumping together during cooking.

Meanwhile, add one small ladle of stock to the rice and stir occasionally, until the stock has been absorbed by the rice. Keep doing this until the rice is *al dente* (that is, has a slight firmness to it). Add the cream, remaining butter, Parmesan, lemon zest and crab meat. Adjust the seasoning and set aside somewhere warm.

With the fish, which should still be hot after you've removed it from the oven, slice each portion on an angle into about five pieces. Split the risotto into four warm bowls then fan the monkfish pieces in an attractive manner onto the top of each risotto.

Garnish with the chopped chives and either a drizzle of extra virgin olive oil or a white wine and cream reduction. Serve immediately.

PAN-SEARED
Fillet of brill

WITH A WARM NEW POTATO, FENNEL AND GREEN BEAN SALAD AND SAUCE VIERGE

Pan-seared fillet of brill

INGREDIENTS

4 x 150g brill portions

Olive oil, for cooking and to taste

800g cooked new potatoes

300g cooked green beans

2 bulbs of fennel, cut into wedges and roasted

12 kalamata olives, quartered

Juice of 1 lemon

Salt and pepper, to season

Unsalted butter, for cooking (optional)

For the sauce vierge:

Zest of 1 lemon and juice of half

1 orange, segmented and diced

1 tbsp chopped parsley

Half tbsp chopped chives

Half tbsp chopped basil

1 banana shallot, finely diced

25g Lilliput capers

1 vine tomato, skinned, deseeded and diced

100ml olive oil

Salt and pepper, to season

You will also need:

A non-stick frying pan

METHOD

Mix the potatoes, beans, fennel and olives in a bowl and add olive oil and lemon juice to taste. Season with salt and pepper and set aside.

For the sauce, add all the ingredients except salt and pepper together and then season to taste. If you're going to use it straight away, leave out at room temperature. It will keep in a fridge for at least 3 days, as long as the oil covers all the ingredients.

In a non-stick frying pan over a medium to high heat, add a splash of olive oil. Season the fish fillets with salt and pepper and carefully lay them into the hot oil. Add a few knobs of butter for colour on the fish and richness (this is optional). The fish will take roughly 2-3 minutes either side, depending on the thickness of the fish.

When cooked, remove the fish from the pan and place on a plate somewhere warm. Stir the salad ingredients into the juices in the pan to warm through.

To serve, split the salad between four warm plates or bowls. Serve the fish next to the salad, spoon over a little of the sauce and serve the remaining sauce in a bowl or jug for your guests to help themselves to if they want more.

Sea bass en papillotte

WITH AROMATIC VEGETABLES AND A CITRUS BUTTER SAUCE

Serves 4

INGREDIENTS

4 x 200g sea bass fillets

2 medium-sized carrots, finely sliced

2 bulbs fennel, finely sliced

1 leek, cleaned, trimmed and finely sliced

20g ginger, peeled and finely sliced

1 red onion, peeled and finely sliced

Half tsp chopped thyme

Half celeriac, finely sliced

1 clove garlic, finely chopped

Splash of white wine

Drizzle of olive oil

Salt and pepper, to season

For the sauce:

Juice of 1 lemon

Fennel fronds – the top parts of the bulbs

2 chopped banana shallots

2 cloves chopped garlic

100ml dry sweet white wine

20ml white wine vinegar

4 peppercorns

1 bay leaf

1 sprig thyme

200g diced unsalted butter

1 tomato, peeled and diced

50ml double cream

1 tsp chopped chives

You will also need:

Foil

Baking parchment

Continued on the next page...

 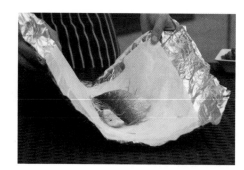 

METHOD

Make the sauce first as it will hold at room temperature until you're ready to serve the dish. In a stainless steel pan, add all the sauce ingredients except the butter, tomato, cream and chives, and reduce over a medium heat until nearly all the liquid has evaporated. Stir in the cream and simmer again until it has become very thick – after about 5 minutes.

Get your cold diced butter (reserving four small pieces, about 5g each, for the cooking of the fish) and whisk it all into the cream. Other recipes will say to do this gradually but there's no need. Pass the sauce through a fine sieve, season to taste and set aside.

Pre-heat the oven to 180 degrees centigrade then lay out four pieces of foil large enough to envelop the fish. Lay a piece of parchment paper on top of each, making sure it is slightly smaller than the foil.

In a bowl, add the carrots, fennel, leek, ginger, onion, thyme, celeriac and garlic and add a splash of white wine and a drizzle of olive oil. Season well with salt and pepper and split between the four pieces of parchment paper. Season the sea bass and place a fillet on top of each of the piles of vegetables, then put the butter you reserved on top of each piece of fish.

Pull the sides of the foil up and crimp them together tightly so the steam won't escape. Place the parcels on a baking tray and straight into the oven for 12-18 minutes. To check if the fish is cooked, just unwrap one of the parcels, carefully so the steam doesn't burn you, and with a spoon handle press at the flesh of the fish. If it's soft and starts to flake off when you press it, it's cooked. If not, cook for a little longer and check again. Meanwhile, warm four plates in the oven.

When the fish is out of the oven, return the butter sauce to a saucepan over a low heat to warm. Don't let the sauce boil as it will split. When it's warm, stir in the tomato and chopped chives.

Carefully unwrap the fish and lift the bass fillet off. Remove the warmed plates from the oven, carefully arrange the vegetables in the centre of each plate and put the bass back on top of them. Pour some sauce around and slightly over the fish and vegetables and serve. Alternatively, you could serve in the parcels as shown in the picture opposite.

New potatoes are a good choice with this simple fish dish if you want a larger meal. If you want to make the parcels in advance, they will keep in a fridge for 24 hours before cooking, but no longer as the vegetables will sweat and discolour.

salads

Chargrilled vegetable salad

Serves 4

INGREDIENTS

1 red pepper

1 yellow pepper

20 cherry vine tomatoes

Extra virgin olive oil, for cooking

Salt and pepper, to season and to

salt the aubergine

1 aubergine

2 courgettes

1 x 385g tin artichoke hearts

Chopped basil, thyme and rosemary,

to dress

2 cloves chopped garlic

8 cooked baby leeks

12 spears of cooked asparagus

2 red onions, peeled and cut into wedges

4 peeled field mushrooms

1 x 200g bag washed baby spinach

Aged balsamic vinegar (optional)

METHOD

Pre-heat the oven to 200 degrees centigrade. Put the peppers and cherry tomatoes on a baking tray, drizzle with olive oil and seasoning and put into the oven. When the peppers' skins are blistered, remove from the oven, put them in a bowl, cover with clingfilm and leave them for 5 minutes – this will make the skins easier to peel. Leave the tomatoes on the tray as you can use this tray to reheat the other ingredients before serving. Pre-heat either a chargrill or light a barbecue if you prefer, then cut your aubergine, courgettes and artichokes into slices of about 50mm thickness. Salt the aubergine lightly and leave in a colander for roughly 30 minutes to soften it and remove any bitterness. Peel and deseed your peppers and cut them into quarters. Mix your chopped herbs and garlic with enough olive oil until you get a thick herb dressing. Wash your sliced vegetables, leeks, asparagus, onions and mushrooms, and pat them dry, then pour the herb dressing over them. Season well with salt and pepper and allow to marinate for 15-30 minutes at room temperature.

When your grill/barbecue is hot, chargrill your vegetables in batches: aubergines first, then courgettes and so on. Place them on the tray with your tomatoes ready to reheat the salad before serving.

Place your salad items back into the oven until warm, then put them into a large bowl and mix the baby spinach leaves through – they will wilt down with the residual heat. Split the vegetables between 4 serving bowls or plates, and arrange nicely with your leeks and asparagus on the top.

Finish the salad with a drizzle of balsamic vinegar if you like, and maybe a few freshly chopped herbs.

Chargrilled tuna niçoise

Serves 4

INGREDIENTS

4 x 170-226g (6-8oz) tuna steaks
200g cooked green beans
20 pitted black olives, halved
20 cherry vine tomatoes, quartered
200g cooked new potatoes, quartered
8 anchovies, cut into small pieces
1 medium-sized red onion, peeled and
thinly sliced
4 soft boiled eggs, peeled
100g washed mixed salad leaves
1 tbsp chopped fresh parsley, to
garnish (optional)

For the salad dressing:
75ml extra virgin olive oil
30ml good quality balsamic vinegar
Half clove crushed garlic
50g diced tomato (just the flesh, not the seeds)
Salt and ground black pepper, to season

You will also need:
A griddle pan or heavy-based frying pan

METHOD

Pour a little of the olive oil for the salad dressing over the tuna steaks, season with salt and ground black pepper and leave covered to get to room temperature.

Put the griddle pan or frying pan over a medium to high heat to get hot.

Put all the salad ingredients into a bowl, except the boiled eggs and the salad leaves. You want to add these at the last minute or they will wilt.

In a separate bowl, add all the dressing ingredients and whisk them together. Season with salt and pepper and pour the majority over the salad ingredients, reserving a little to drizzle over the finished dish just before serving.

Carefully place your tuna onto the griddle pan and cook for roughly 2 minutes either side, depending on the thickness of the fish. If you don't like your tuna served pink then cook it for longer.

Mix the salad leaves in with the rest of the salad ingredients and arrange carefully on four plates or larger bowls. Place the tuna on top of each of the salads, cut the boiled eggs into quarters or halves and arrange around the tuna. Drizzle the remaining dressing over, garnish with the chopped parsley if desired and serve.

Chicken Caesar salad

Serves 4

INGREDIENTS

For the dressing:

1 and a half garlic cloves, crushed

1 whole egg

1 egg yolk

1 tsp chopped gherkins

2 tsp chopped capers

100g finely grated Parmesan

4 crushed anchovy fillets

Juice of 1 lemon

10 drops Tabasco sauce

2 tsp Dijon mustard

3 tsp Worcestershire sauce

2 tbsp cold water

300ml vegetable oil

100ml olive oil

Salt and pepper, to taste

METHOD

Mix all of the ingredients (excluding the oils and water) in a Robot Coupe/food processor until a smooth paste is achieved. If the paste is very thick, add a few drops of the water to loosen the dressing, as this will allow it to be combined much easier.

Start to add the oils (it doesn't matter which one first), very slowly to begin with. Do this whilst the processor is running, in exactly the same way as you would with a mayonnaise. If you add the oil too quickly, the dressing will split. If the dressing is getting too thick or too shiny, which is an indication that the dressing may split, then add a little more of the water and this will rectify the problem.

When all of the oil has been added, adjust the seasoning to your own particular taste. If the dressing is a little thin then more oil can be added at this stage until the desired consistency is reached.

Continued on the next page...

INGREDIENTS

For the salad:

Quarter of Romaine lettuce per person (discard the bitter-tasting dark green outer leaves)

1 poached chicken breast per person (sliced into decent-size pieces)

Crisp croutons (either baked or pan-fried, depending on preference)

30g Parmesan per person (15g finely grated, 15g shaved)

4-8 brown salted anchovies per person

4-8 pitted black olives per person

Caesar salad dressing, to taste

METHOD

Rip the romaine leaves into 5 centimetre (2 inch) pieces and place into a suitable size bowl, along with the grated and shaved Parmesan, croutons, anchovies and chicken breast and a little of the Caesar dressing. Reserve enough of the croutons, chicken, anchovies and shaved Parmesan to garnish the finished salad with.

Move all the salad items around gently so that the lettuce doesn't get bruised, and add more dressing as desired to your own preference.

Arrange the salad in a nice presentation bowl and carefully place all the reserved items on top of the salad to make it appealing to the eye. Serve a little of the remaining dressing on the side.

If you have dressing left over, it can be kept in a fridge for up to 3 days, but no longer because of the raw egg it contains.

Pasta

Field mushroom linguine

Serves 4

WITH RED PEPPER AND CHILLI

INGREDIENTS

Splash of olive oil, for cooking

100g shallot, finely diced

2 cloves chopped garlic

1 diced mild red chilli

250g red pepper, finely sliced

40g unsalted butter

250g field mushrooms, peeled and sliced

100g sliced button or wild mushrooms

Salt and pepper, to season

50ml medium dry white wine

300ml double cream

400g cooked linguine pasta

10g chopped tarragon

10g chopped parsley

100g finely grated Parmesan

METHOD

In a heavy-based pan, add the olive oil, shallot, garlic and chilli and sweat off for a couple of minutes. Add the red pepper and cook until tender – about 2-3 minutes. Turn up the heat and add the butter.

When the butter is foaming, add the mushrooms and season with salt and pepper. When the mushrooms are tender, add the white wine and reduce until the wine has nearly evaporated.

Add the double cream and simmer until the sauce has started to thicken – about 2-3 minutes. Add the cooked linguine pasta, tarragon, parsley and half the grated Parmesan. Adjust the seasoning to taste.

Serve and sprinkle with the remaining Parmesan cheese.

Penne pasta

WITH CHORIZO AND SMOKED BACON IN A SPICY TOMATO SAUCE

INGREDIENTS

50ml olive oil

2 diced red onions

4 cloves garlic, peeled and chopped

1-2 chopped red chillies (depending on desired heat)

200g diced chorizo picante

100g smoked bacon lardons

40ml standard balsamic vinegar

200ml water

50g tomato purée

2 x 400g tins chopped tomatoes

300g dried penne pasta

Salt and pepper, to season

Chilli flakes, to taste (optional)

100g grated or shaved Parmesan

100g rocket leaves (optional)

METHOD

In a heavy-based saucepan on a medium heat, add your olive oil, red onion, garlic and chilli and sweat off without colour.

In a separate frying pan on a high heat, add your chorizo – you want to crisp the chorizo and release the oils. After a minute or two, add your bacon lardons to the chorizo and sauté them together until crisp.

Deglaze the pan with the balsamic vinegar and a splash of the water then add this into your pan with the onions. Add the tomato purée and cook it over a medium heat for a few minutes, stirring occasionally to avoid burning the base of the pan. Add your chopped tomatoes and the remaining water and simmer for roughly 30 minutes or until a nice thick consistency is achieved.

Cook your pasta according to the packet instructions, then strain and add to your sauce.

Adjust the seasoning – you want to do this at the end just before serving, as the bacon and chorizo are both well-seasoned. If you want a little more spice in the sauce, add a few chilli flakes.

Divide into four bowls, sprinkle with the Parmesan and garnish with the rocket leaves if you like.

Something
Special

For many of us, cooking is a chore – an enjoyable one, yes, but a means to an end all the same. With our busy modern lifestyles, we mostly tend to favour simple dishes and a casual approach to dining. But every once in a while, it's nice to treat ourselves to something more – something special.

Much of the food served at Casa is simple, but we're more than capable of catering for special occasions as well. That could be for one of the many wedding receptions we host at the hotel, or just guests sharing a birthday or anniversary celebration in the Cocina Restaurant.

In this section, you'll find some of our favourite recipes for these special occasions. These dishes, with their big flavours and indulgent ingredients, will add the 'wow' factor to a dinner party, romantic night in or other treasured occasion. They may take slightly longer to prepare than some of the other recipes in the book, but the results will truly be special.

Of course, when preparing a special meal, you need something special to accompany it. A great bottle of wine can provide the finishing touch that will make your dinner one to remember.

To offer a helping hand and give us some suitably special suggestions, we've asked local wine merchant John Hattersley. His incredible expertise comes from a lifelong passion for wine, and years of experience in the industry.

John has a particular connection with Casa's Spanish-inspired ethos, as his father had a bar in Torremolinos in the 1960s. He spent summers surrounded by tapas, learning instinctively which wines went with which kinds of food – zesty whites for seafood, fruity reds for richer dishes and so on.

Later, John spent many years running popular wine bars and restaurants across Derbyshire and South Yorkshire. In 2004, John Hattersley Wines was established. What began as a passion project for John's semi-retirement is now a thriving retail and trade business, with customers from far and wide seeking out John and his team for their vast knowledge of wine.

John is educated to diploma level with the Wine & Spirit Trust, and regularly visits wine producers to keep up with current trends and developments in the industry. His philosophy is that wine is not just a bottle with a price tag, but an experience to be savoured.

You could say much the same about food. John has selected a wine to accompany each dish in this section, as well as others elsewhere in the book. Together, they're a match made in heaven.

Read more about John and his team and browse their fabulous selection of wines at www.johnhwines.co.uk.

Walton Lodge pork belly

WITH A ROOT VEGETABLE SAUERKRAUT, POTATO FONDANT AND A RED WINE AND APPLE SAUCE

Serves 4-6

Although this may seem like a lot of work, this is an ideal dish for a dinner party as all the preparation is done the day before and serving the dish is relatively simple.

INGREDIENTS

For the dry rub:

50g Maldon salt

Zest of 1 orange

2 chopped cloves garlic

20g chopped rosemary

20g chopped thyme

20g dried lavender

20g whole dried chillies, chopped and deseeded

METHOD

Combine all these ingredients in a bowl then massage all over the pork belly. Leave the pork on a lipped tray (as the salt will draw moisture from the pork) at either room temperature for 3 hours or in a fridge for 12 hours.

Continued on the next page...

Walton Lodge pork belly

INGREDIENTS

For the pork belly:

Allow 8oz/226g of raw pork belly per person. Use a good quality outdoor-reared pork – this will give you a deeper joint of pork which will work better for this dish, as you will lose a percentage of the size due to the confit cooking process.

We use pork from our own farm but a good quality butcher will steer you in the right direction. 900g-1.35kg pork belly, depending on how many people you are serving (left whole for the confit stage of cooking)

2 chopped cloves garlic

20g chopped rosemary

20g chopped thyme

20g dried lavender

20g dried chilli

500g goose fat

1 litre vegetable oil

METHOD

Pre-heat the oven to 140 degrees centigrade.

Wash the dry rub off the pork in cold water and dry well with kitchen paper. Heat the oil and goose fat with the other ingredients in a deep-sided baking tray in the oven to infuse the flavours into the oil. Don't get the oil too hot or the garlic will colour and make the oil bitter.

When the goose fat has melted, carefully lower the pork into the oil/fat, cover with tin foil and place in the pre-heated oven. The pork will take roughly 3 hours, but after 2½ hours remove from the oven and press the flesh of the pork belly with a carving fork to see if it is tender enough. The pork should feel delicate, almost as if it will tear apart. If it is not, return to the oven for the remaining cooking time.

When tender, remove the tray from the oven and leave the pork to cool in the oil until it is at a safe temperature to handle, then remove from the oil/fat and place on a greaseproof paper-lined lipped baking sheet. Place another sheet of greaseproof paper on top of the pork. Put a flat tray on top of this and add weight to it (roughly 6 cans of beans will suffice). Leave for at least 4 hours or preferably overnight in the fridge. This will press the pork into a nice shape so that it will present well when serving, and also remove any excess fat.

Reserve the cooking oil to cook the fondant potatoes in.

A recommendation from John Hattersley Wines:

"This Walton Lodge belly pork, with its chilli and lavender scent, needs a big white wine with attitude, and I think the **Macià Batle Blanco** from Mallorca will suit perfectly. The breadth of flavours from the Chardonnay will match the pork, a little oak ageing gives the wine structure and the indigenous Prensal Blanc grape adds fruit to complement the sweetness in the apple sauce."

INGREDIENTS

For the sauerkraut:
2 shallots, finely sliced
2 crushed cloves garlic
Half red cabbage, finely shredded
2 carrots, cut into fine strips or grated
100ml cider vinegar
50g white sugar
Juice of half lemon
20g chopped thyme
Half spring cabbage, finely shredded
Salt and pepper, to season

For the fondant potato:
6 medium-sized Maris Piper potatoes
Oil and goose fat mixture, retained from the pork belly cooking stage (enough to cover the potatoes)
50g butter
Maldon salt, to season
1 bay leaf
6 peppercorns
1 clove garlic, peeled and chopped
4 sprigs thyme

METHOD

Sweat off the shallot and garlic in a saucepan until translucent. Add the red cabbage and carrot and cook until *al dente* – approximately 5 minutes.

Deglaze the pan with the cider vinegar and reduce the liquid by half. Add the sugar, lemon juice and chopped thyme and bring to a simmer.

Remove from the heat, stir in the raw spring cabbage and season to taste with salt and pepper. Place in a bowl whilst still hot, cover with clingfilm and when cooled place in the fridge for at least 24 hours to ferment.

Cut the potatoes to the desired shape. We do a rectangle but any shape is fine as long as it has a flat base and top, and all the potatoes are of an equal size so that they cook evenly.

In a little of the reserved oil and goose fat mixture in a saucepan, fry the potatoes on both sides until a nice golden brown.

Season well then cover with the remaining fat. Add the bay leaf, peppercorns, garlic and thyme to the pan. Add the butter and cook the potatoes at a light simmer until they are cooked all the way through – about 45 minutes.

Continued on the next page...

Walton Lodge pork belly

INGREDIENTS

For the chilli and lavender glaze:

75ml honey

10g lavender seeds

1 red chilli, deseeded and finely chopped

Heat all the ingredients in a saucepan and simmer until all the flavours have infused – about 5 minutes.

For the red wine and apple sauce:

Splash of vegetable oil, for cooking

1 chopped carrot

2 sticks chopped celery

4 chopped large shallots

500ml red wine

1 bay leaf

3 sprigs thyme

3 peppercorns

50ml port

50ml Madeira

1.14 litres (2 pints) fresh beef stock (we make our own but supermarkets sell good quality beef stock)

50g diced cold butter

1 Granny Smith apple, peeled and finely diced

50g chives, finely chopped

METHOD

Heat a thick-based sauté pan then add a splash of vegetable oil. Add the carrot, celery and shallots – you want to colour them but not burn them.

When nicely browned, add the red wine, bay leaf, thyme and peppercorns and bring to the boil. Reduce the wine until it has nearly evaporated then add the port and Madeira.

Boil for a minute or so to remove the bitter alcohol flavour and then add the beef stock. Reduce until the sauce is thickened to the desired consistency – roughly that of single cream. This should take about 10 minutes.

Pass the vegetables out of the liquid through a fine sieve and press down on them with the back of a ladle so as to get all the flavour out of them. When ready to serve, bring the sauce back to the boil and whisk in the cold butter – this will give the sauce a nice glossy finish and a velvety mouthfeel.

Add the diced apple and chives just before serving.

TO SERVE

Cut the pork belly into the desired portion sizes, keeping them all the same size for even cooking. Pre-heat the oven to 180 degrees centigrade.

Place the potatoes on greaseproof paper and place in the oven for roughly 10 minutes or until hot all the way through. In a frying pan, fry the pork belly on all sides until golden brown and then place on the same tray as the potatoes in the oven. Baste with the chilli and lavender glaze and leave until heated through thoroughly – about 10 minutes.

Warm the sauerkraut on the stove and check the seasoning. Finish the red wine and apple sauce with butter as mentioned earlier.

We serve the dish with a few pieces of purple sprouting broccoli but French beans would be a good alternative.

Saddle of Walton Lodge new season lamb

Serves 4

WITH BROAD BEANS, PEAS AND A REDCURRANT AND ROSEMARY JUS

INGREDIENTS

400g boneless lamb shoulder

Salt and pepper, to season and for cooking the peas and beans

4 cloves garlic, peeled and chopped

1 litre duck fat, or chicken stock if you prefer to braise rather than confit the shoulder

500g peeled Maris Piper potatoes

200ml double cream

75g unsalted butter

100g grated Parmesan

4 x 200g portions lamb saddle (ask your butcher to bone and roll the lamb for you) – we use Walton Lodge lamb

100g fresh peas – frozen will do if you can't get fresh

100g fresh broad beans – frozen will do if you can't get fresh

Water, for cooking

12 baby carrots, peeled and cooked

For the sauce:

Rapeseed oil, for cooking

1 sprig rosemary

100g chopped shallot

2 sticks chopped celery

2 cloves garlic

1 carrot, peeled and chopped

1 bay leaf

4 peppercorns

500ml red wine

100ml port

1 litre fresh lamb or beef stock

30g redcurrant jelly

Salt and pepper, to season

METHOD

Pre-heat the oven to 140 degrees centigrade.

Season the lamb shoulder with salt and pepper and place in an ovenproof dish.

Add the garlic then pour over the duck fat or hot chicken stock if you're braising it. Make sure the lamb is totally submerged in the liquid. Cover the dish with foil and place into the oven. The lamb will take roughly 90 minutes to cook. You want it to be so tender it is falling apart, so if this isn't happening return it to the oven until it is. When it is tender, remove from the oven, allow to cool then flake all the meat down, removing any fat. Place to one side.

Cook the potatoes in salted water until cooked all the way through. Drain into a colander, allow all the steam to evaporate then mash.

Put the cream, butter and Parmesan into a pan, stir together and simmer until the cream has become thick. Slowly beat the cream into the potatoes a little at a time – you don't want the mash to be too runny. Season and set to one side.

In a heavy-bottomed saucepan over a medium to high heat, add a little oil and all the sauce ingredients except the liquids and redcurrant jelly. Colour them well, being careful not to let them burn.

When you have a nice brown colour to the vegetables – after about 10 minutes – add the red wine and allow this to reduce until the wine has nearly all evaporated. Add the port and repeat the process.

When the port is nearly gone, add the stock and redcurrant jelly and again reduce the liquid until it has thickened to a sauce-like consistency. Pass the sauce through a fine sieve, pressing down the vegetables well so you get all the flavour from them. Season and set aside till plating.

For the saddle, turn the oven up to 180 degrees centigrade. Season the meat with salt and pepper. In a frying pan, render down as much fat as you can from the outside of the lamb. When it is a nice golden brown, place on a baking tray and put into the oven for roughly 8 minutes, turning once or twice during cooking.

After the 8 minutes are up, press the meat of the saddle with your finger. It should feel the same as a medium-cooked steak – that is, the meat should be tender but should 'spring back' when pressed rather than leaving an indent. If so, remove from the oven and leave it somewhere warm for the meat to relax.

Cook the peas and broad beans in boiling salted water until tender and drain them when cooked. Place the lamb shoulder into the still-hot oven to heat and crisp up slightly – about 3-4 minutes. Reheat the mashed potato and the lamb sauce.

When the shoulder is hot, add it to the peas and broad beans and keep them warm.

Heat the baby carrots up in the lamb sauce, slice each piece of lamb saddle into 3 even pieces and then serve as shown in the photo. In the restaurant we pipe the mash onto the plate, but this is not essential.

A recommendation from John Hattersley Wines:

"To complement the saddle of Walton Lodge lamb, with its redcurrant and rosemary jus, I would recommend the **Valenciso Rioja Reserva**, voted the Fine Wine of the Year 2014 by the Guild of Sommeliers in London. Lamb and Rioja make a heavenly match – there is just something about the softness in the lamb that is complemented by the delicate fruit flavours of a quality Rioja with light integrated oak."

Saddle of Walton Lodge new season lamb with broad beans, peas and a redcurrant and rosemary jus

Roast duck with a celeriac purée, grilled asparagus, roasted new potatoes and a red wine and cherry jus

Roast duck

WITH A CELERIAC PURÉE, GRILLED ASPARAGUS, ROASTED NEW POTATOES AND A RED WINE AND CHERRY JUS

INGREDIENTS

4 x duck breasts, roughly 200-250g each – try to get female breasts if possible, as these are more tender

1 celeriac, peeled and evenly diced

1 chopped banana shallot

2 cloves garlic, peeled and chopped

1 sprig thyme

200ml whole milk

100ml double cream

Salt and pepper, to season plus more to cook the potatoes

12 large new potatoes – around 200g

20 spears asparagus, cooked, refreshed in ice water and drained

Water, for cooking

Oil, for cooking the asparagus

16 pitted cherries

For the sauce:

Oil, for cooking

100g chopped shallot

2 sticks chopped celery

2 cloves garlic

1 carrot, peeled and chopped

1 bay leaf

4 peppercorns

500ml red wine

100ml port

1 litre duck or beef stock

30g redcurrant jelly

Salt and pepper, to season

You will also need:

A griddle pan

Baking parchment

Saucepan – stainless steel if possible

METHOD

For the sauce:

In a heavy-bottomed saucepan over a medium to high heat, add a little oil and all the sauce ingredients except the liquids and redcurrant jelly. Colour them well, being careful not to let them burn. When you have a nice brown colour to the vegetables – after about 10 minutes – add the red wine and allow this to reduce until the wine has nearly all evaporated. Add the port and repeat the process. When the port is nearly gone, add the stock and redcurrant jelly and again reduce the liquid until it has thickened to a sauce consistency. Pass the sauce through a fine sieve, pressing down the vegetables well so you get all the flavour from them. Season and set aside till plating.

For the dish:

Heat the oven to 180 degrees centigrade.

In a saucepan, add your celeriac, shallot, garlic, thyme, milk and double cream, stirring occasionally, and bring to the boil. Turn down to a simmer and cover with baking parchment, pressing the parchment down so that all the celeriac is submerged, and cook until tender – about 15-20 minutes.

When cooked, drain the celeriac into a colander (if you reserve the liquid, it can be used either in a soup or perhaps a celeriac-flavoured dauphinoise potato). Whilst the celeriac is still warm, purée it in a food processor and pass through a sieve to remove any lumps. Adjust the seasoning and set aside until needed.

Peel or turn the new potatoes and bring to the boil in salted water. Simmer them for about 5 minutes, drain them into a colander and set aside. Season your duck breasts and place them skin side down into a cold frying pan. Place the pan over a medium heat and cook on the skin side until the fat has rendered down and the skin is starting to become a light golden brown – around 3 minutes. Turn them onto the flesh side to seal the meat and then turn them back skin side down.

Add your new potatoes to the same pan and toss/stir them in the fat. Place into the oven for roughly 8 minutes, or until the duck is cooked to your liking. If the new potatoes need longer, remove the duck from the pan and return the potatoes to the oven until they are cooked through. Rub the asparagus with oil, season well and put onto a warm griddle pan to heat through, allowing it to get bar marks from the pan. Reheat your sauce and add the cherries to warm through, reheat the purée and new potatoes.

Slice the duck breasts and serve as shown in the photo on the previous page.

A recommendation from John Hattersley Wines:
"The richness of this roast duck, with the sweetness of the cherry jus, will be enhanced by one of our best wines, the **Tres Picos** from Borsao, a 100 per cent Grenache from Campo de Borja, south east of Rioja. The dense flavours of blackcurrant and strawberry fruits, combined with the long sweet tannins, are perfect to accompany this rich dish. No wonder it is one of leading wine critic Robert Parker's favourite wines."

109

Tapas

A recommendation from
John Hattersley Wines:
"These tapas would be
well received with a chilled
glass of **Fernando di
Castilla Fino** sherry."

Albondigas con tomate

INGREDIENTS

For the albondigas (meatballs):

Olive oil, for cooking

226g (8oz) minced pork or beef

50g fresh breadcrumbs

3 cloves finely chopped garlic

50g finely grated manchego cheese

2 sprigs fresh thyme, picked and finely
chopped

15g hot paprika

Salt and pepper, to season

1 beaten egg

For the sauce:

Olive oil, for cooking

1 onion, peeled and finely diced

1 stick celery, peeled and finely diced

2 cloves peeled and chopped garlic

1 medium-hot red chilli, deseeded and
finely chopped

1 bay leaf

100ml red wine

2 x 400g tins chopped tomatoes

METHOD

Start with the sauce: in a saucepan, add a splash of olive oil followed by the onion, celery, garlic, chilli and bay leaf and sweat off until soft. Add the wine and reduce till the pan is nearly dry. Add the chopped tomatoes and simmer for 20-30 minutes.

In a large bowl, add all the meatball ingredients and mix either with a spoon or with clean hands until the ingredients are combined completely. Season to taste (Tip: fry a little of the meatball mix to check the seasoning and adjust to taste).

Shape into 16-20 balls and place in the fridge for 20 minutes to firm up. When firm, put a pan onto the heat – either use a pan big enough to fit all of the meatballs in, or do them in smaller batches. Add a little olive oil and fry the meatballs for a few minutes until they are nicely browned.

Add the meatballs to your sauce, which should have started to thicken by now, and simmer for roughly 20 minutes or until the meatballs are cooked through.

Taste, and season accordingly. Serve either with or without crusty bread.

Chef's tip: Serve with spaghetti as a main course rather than a tapas.

Cajun calamari

Serves 4

INGREDIENTS

2 crushed garlic cloves
100ml good quality mayonnaise
20g chopped parsley
12.5g baking powder
25g Cajun seasoning
*150g cornflour (100g for the batter, 50g
for coating the squid)*
400ml ice cold soda water
*500g baby squid, cleaned and sliced
into rings*
1 lemon, cut into quarters

You will also need:
A deep-fat fryer
*Rapeseed oil, for cooking – enough to fill
the fryer*

METHOD

Mix the garlic, mayonnaise and chopped parsley together and put into 4 small ramekins. In a bowl, add your baking powder, Cajun seasoning and 200g of cornflour. Pre-heat your fryer to 180 degrees centigrade.

At the last minute, add the soda water to the cornflour mix and whisk until it has reached a consistency similar to single cream. Don't overwork the batter – a few lumps are fine. Dust the squid with the remaining cornflour – this will allow the batter to stick to the squid itself. Dip in the batter, remove it and allow any excess batter to fall off the squid. Lower the squid gently into the oil. Keep it moving at all times whilst in the oil, otherwise it will clump together and not be crisp. Fry the squid in small batches or the oil will cool down and make the squid soggy.

Serve on plates with a lemon wedge and the dipping dish of garlic mayonnaise.

Gambas pil pil

Serves 4

INGREDIENTS

800g raw prawns, peeled and deveined

10g salt

80ml olive oil

50g unsalted butter

5g dried chilli flakes

3 chopped garlic cloves

10g paprika

This is a simple tapas classic, but if done well it's delicious.

METHOD

Firstly, season the prawns with the salt and leave at room temperature for about 20 minutes. In a sauté pan over a medium heat, add the olive oil and butter. When the butter is foaming, add the chilli and garlic and cook for about a minute. Don't let the garlic colour too much as it will taste bitter.

Add the prawns and cook for 3-4 minutes or until they change colour and firm up slightly. Add the paprika and pour into 4 tapas dishes.

Serve with rustic bread to dip into the spicy oil and butter mixture to fully enjoy the dish.

Hake, cheese & chive croquettes

Serves 4

INGREDIENTS

600g hake fillet, pin-boned and skinned

568ml (1 pint) milk

1 bay leaf

3 peppercorns

Salt and pepper, to season

1 large baked potato (interior scooped out, mashed and kept warm)

60g grated strong white cheddar

125g chopped gherkins

125g chopped capers

20g chopped chives

Zest of 1 lemon

20g chopped parsley

For the panne (coating):

100g Panko breadcrumbs

2 eggs

75g plain flour

Aioli or tomato salsa, to serve

You will also need:

A deep fat fryer

Oil, for cooking

METHOD

In a pan large enough to place the fish into, add the milk, bay leaf, peppercorns and a good pinch of salt and bring the milk to a simmer. Carefully place the fish into the milk and simmer for a couple of minutes until the fish is cooked (basically when you can separate the flakes of fish).

Strain into a colander over a bowl so you retain the milk underneath. Let the fish cool slightly so that you can handle it and flake the fish into a bowl with your mashed baked potato (make sure the potato is still warm at this stage).

Add the cheddar, gherkins, capers, chives, lemon zest and chopped parsley into the bowl. Mix thoroughly but try not to completely mash the fish.

Check the seasoning and roll into balls. Try to get 12 even-sized balls out of this mix, although you can make larger or smaller balls if you like. Place the croquettes on a tray and place in the fridge for 30 minutes to firm up.

Get three small bowls. Into one place the flour, in the second place the breadcrumbs and in the third crack the eggs. Break these up with a fork and add a little of the milk you saved earlier to thin out the liquid.

Place two or three of the croquettes into the flour then lift them out and shake off the excess. Put them into the egg and milk mix, lift them out and remove the excess. Finally, place them into the breadcrumbs, ensuring they get a good coating all round. Place them on a tray and repeat with the other croquettes until they are all coated. Return them to the fridge for 30 minutes to firm up again.

Heat your fryer to 180 degrees centigrade and lower the croquettes carefully into the oil. Cook until they are a nice golden brown and are hot in the centre – roughly 6 minutes. Serve with aioli or a tomato salsa.

Pan con tomate

Serves 4

This is another really simple dish, but as long as you have great ripe tomatoes it's also very tasty. It can be served with various accompaniments like salads for a bit of crunch or just on its own for a simple starter. If you add some good quality serrano ham or thinly-sliced manchego cheese, it makes a great simple lunch.

INGREDIENTS

4 slices crusty bread or baguette (slightly stale is fine)

1 clove peeled garlic

2 very ripe vine or plum tomatoes, at room temperature

Extra virgin olive oil, to serve

Salt, to season

METHOD

Slice and toast the bread – not too thinly – and rub generously with the raw garlic.

Cut your tomatoes (which should be at room temperature to improve the flavour) in half and rub the cut side across your toasted bread, squashing and rubbing in the tomato as you do so.

Drizzle with olive oil, season with a little salt and serve.

Pimientos de Padrón

Serves 4

INGREDIENTS

400g pimientos de Padrón, rinsed in water
60ml olive oil
50g Maldon salt flakes

METHOD

This is an incredibly simple dish but also one of the more commonly available and traditional tapas. Roughly one in ten of the peppers are incredibly hot which makes this a great dish to share with friends, as when someone eats one of the spicy peppers the reaction is normally quite hilarious.

You want a good heavy-based sauté pan. Get the pan on your burner as high as it will go, and when the pan is hot, add the oil and straight away add the peppers and the majority of the salt. You want the pepper skins to blister and colour to an even golden brown.

As soon as the peppers are tender – after about 3 minutes – transfer them to your serving dish and scatter with the remaining salt. They are ideal with cold beer, as this is a true bar tapas.

Charcutería

No wonder the Spanish love charcutería so much. When you're sat in the sun with an ice cold cerveza, there really is no finer accompaniment than some succulent, salty ham.

Charcutería – the collective term for various types of prepared meat product – is an integral part of the Spanish diet. Whether cured sausages like chorizo or salchichón, or ham like the famous jamón ibérico, its popularity is unwavering.

Charcutería is a common ingredient in many Spanish and Spanish-inspired dishes. But their distinctive flavours are good enough for them to be enjoyed on their own as well, as a tapas meal or just a simple, delicious snack.

Of course, to be able to enjoy charcutería in this way, quality is of paramount importance – as with any ingredient, you want the best you can get. At Casa, the goal is to offer guests an authentic Spanish experience, and that means sourcing the finest of the country's charcutería.

Javier De La Hormaza of Grey's Fine Foods

Fortunately, that task is made a lot easier thanks to Javier De La Hormaza of Grey's Fine Foods. Javier is another of our wonderful suppliers, and he shares with Casa a love of food and a personal connection with Spain. Javier is a Spanish-born chef, with a huge passion for his home country's cuisine. His company, founded in Yorkshire in 2012, supplies quality products sourced directly from Spain.

Javier worked in Michelin star restaurants and with various hospitality businesses, before deciding to branch out and start importing fabulous Spanish produce to the UK. He travelled all over Spain for more than a year, meeting with small boutiques and family-run businesses, and these traditional producers now provide Grey's Fine Foods with its unique catalogue of quality goods.

Grey's sources a wide range of charcutería products from across the country but, as Javier insists, nothing rivals Spain's most famous ham – ibérico.

Ibérico ham comes solely from black pigs of the Iberian breed, whose unique origin can be traced back to ancient times. This legendary and select race has many qualities, including a great capacity to accumulate fat under its skin and between its muscular fibres. This fat is what produces the ham's distinctive white streaks, which is what makes it so special.

The main feature that distinguishes ibérico ham from other cured meats is the purity of the breed. The pigs are allowed to move freely around extensive wooded pastures called 'dehesas'. At least a hectare of healthy dehesa is needed to raise a single pig. All pigs are fed on a diet of grass and the best acorns from Holm and Cork Oak meadows, to provide the ham with its distinctive aroma and exquisite taste.

Ibérico hams are generally classified according to the amount of acorns eaten before slaughter. The official classification allowed is distinguished mainly between ibérico de bellota, which are pigs purely fed on acorns, or ibérico de cebo, which are pigs fed on a minor proportion of acorns and a combination of compound feeds approved by the corresponding denomination of origin.

We're big fans of Javier's foodie finds and expertise here at the hotel, but we aren't the only ones who think he's doing a great job. Grey's Fine Foods has won numerous Great Taste Awards, and also supplies to other top restaurants, hotels and delicatessens across the UK.

The name Grey's is a pun on 'graze' – apt, because that's how one should approach eating great charcutería. A nibble here, a small bite there… this is food to be lingered over, to take time with. Sitting in the afternoon sunshine with friends and family, with a bottle of wine open on the table and a plate of great Spanish charcutería in front of you, is one of life's true pleasures. Hopefully after looking at this section of the book, you'll be inspired to sample that pleasure for yourself.

Read more about Javier and Grey's Fine Foods at www.greysfinefoods.com.

1945
ORIGENS
m mas

d'aglà

Acorn fed iberian shoulder
GUIJUELO

m mas
Xoriço Cular
Picant   20,00
Hot Spicy "Chorizo"

m mas
Xoriço ibéric
de Gla (vela)   29,35
Acorn fed iberian chorizo

m mas
Llonganissa
del Montseny   24,90
Special cured sausage

12,35

Pack gou
Embot

CREADORS DE PRODUCTES

Spatlla
bèrica
d'aglà
n fed iberian shoulder
Huelva - Jabugo

m mas
Longaniza con
Pimienta 31,95
Euros/Kg

m mas
LLom ibéric
de Gla 66,75
Acorn fed iberian loin Euros/Kg

m mas
Llonganissa
de Vic 40,05
Special VIC sausage Euros/Kg

16.89 €
20.22 €
20.64 €
25.85 €

Sandv

Barça pepito (steak sandwich)

Serves 1

INGREDIENTS

200g (7oz) 28-day aged rump steak
Olive oil (for the marinade, the salad
dressing and for cooking)
A pinch of paprika
Salt and pepper, to season
1 medium-sized red onion
Pinch of chopped thyme
A splash of port or red wine
A splash of standard balsamic vinegar,
plus more for the salad dressing
Rocket leaves (some for the sandwich and
some to garnish)
1 vine tomato
Ciabatta (or bread of your choice)
Horseradish aioli (garlic and horseradish
mayonnaise), to spread on the sandwich

METHOD

Pre-heat a chargrill or heavy-based frying pan. Marinate your steak with olive oil, paprika, salt and pepper and allow the steak to reach room temperature before cooking.

Prepare your red onion marmalade: slice your onion thinly then add a splash of olive oil to a hot saucepan and put the sliced onion in. Add the chopped thyme and keep stirring so it doesn't burn. When the onion is tender, add a splash of port and reduce the liquid until the port has nearly evaporated. Add a small amount of balsamic vinegar and repeat the reduction process, then season to taste and set aside.

Cook your steak on the chargrill/pan, roughly 2 minutes either side for medium. We wouldn't recommend cooking the steak less than this, as rump steak can be tough if served too pink. When the steak is cooked, set it aside and allow it to rest as this will tenderise the meat and stop all the juices pouring out when you slice it.

Wash your rocket leaves and slice your tomato. To assemble the sandwich, toast your ciabatta and spread the aioli on both sides of the bread. Add your red onion to one side of the ciabatta and then the sliced tomato. Dress your rocket leaves with a little balsamic and olive oil and add some to the sandwich, reserving some of the rocket to garnish the plate with. Finally, slice your steak thinly and arrange evenly through the ciabatta. Place the lid of the sandwich on top and press down firmly, then cut the sandwich in half on an angle and serve either with chips or a few crisps.

Grilled Portobello mushroom

Serves 2

SUN-BLUSHED TOMATO, BUFFALO MOZZARELLA AND ROCKET IN TOASTED SOURDOUGH

INGREDIENTS

2 Portobello mushrooms

A drizzle of extra virgin olive oil

A pinch of chopped lemon thyme

A few knobs of butter

Salt and pepper, to season

100g sliced buffalo mozzarella

2 thick slices of sourdough bread

15g chopped sun-blushed tomato

Dressed rocket leaves, for garnish

1 clove garlic, finely chopped

METHOD

Firstly, pre-heat your grill on its highest temperature and then cover your grill tray with foil. Place the mushrooms on the foil stalk side facing up and drizzle with olive oil, lemon thyme, garlic and a few small knobs of butter and season well with salt and pepper. Place under the grill until tender – approximately 5 minutes – then top them with the buffalo mozzarella and set aside.

Toast the bread on both sides, but grill one side slightly less as when you put the mushrooms on this slice and return it to the grill it will colour more. Place the mushrooms and cheese on the less coloured piece of toast and put it back under the grill until the cheese melts slightly. On the other piece of toast, spread the sun-blushed tomatoes. Add a little of the dressed rocket to the side of the toast, reserving the rest of the leaves for garnish. Put the two sides of the sandwich together, garnish and serve.

Casa club sandwich *Serves 1*

This is a simple sandwich as long as you get all your components ready in advance, such as cooking the chicken and bacon.

INGREDIENTS

3 slices white or brown bread

Butter, to spread on the toast

1 baby gem lettuce, shredded

1 tbsp roasted garlic mayonnaise, mixed with the shredded lettuce

1 sliced soft- or hard-boiled egg, depending on your preference – we serve them soft

1 cooked sliced chicken breast

4 rashers crispy streaky bacon

1 sliced vine tomato

Dressed salad leaves, to garnish

You will also need:

4 cocktail sticks or wooden skewers

METHOD

Toast and butter the bread, ensuring to butter both sides of the middle slice. On the first slice, layer half the lettuce/mayonnaise mix, the soft boiled egg and the sliced chicken breast.

Place the middle slice of bread on top and add the other half of the lettuce, crispy bacon and sliced tomato, then place the remaining slice of toast on top.

Push cocktail sticks or skewers through the toast about 1cm from the edge and halfway down each straight side, so that when you cut the sandwich into quarters on the angle a stick or skewer is holding each quarter together.

Carefully stand each quarter up on its crust edge, and push the sticks or skewers the rest of the way through each quarter of the sandwich to stop the filling from escaping.

Place onto your serving plate and garnish with the dressed salad leaves.

Pudd

Burnt Catalan cream

Serves 6-8

INGREDIENTS

250ml double cream
Zest and juice of 1 orange
Zest and juice of 1 lemon
110g caster sugar, plus more to finish
the dish
4 whole eggs

You will also need:
6-8 ovenproof bowls, about 3cm deep
Chef's blowtorch

METHOD

Pre-heat the oven to 95 degrees centigrade.

Put the cream, orange and lemon juice and zest into a pan and bring up to the boil.

While waiting for cream to boil, mix the sugar and eggs.

Pass the cream through a fine sieve into the sugar mix.

Pour the mix into ovenproof bowls about 1cm deep.

Put into the oven for 35 minutes until nearly firm. The middle of the Catalan should have some movement.

When cooked, leave to one side at room temperature for 30 minutes before refrigerating.

To serve, add 2 tablespoons of caster sugar to the top of the Catalan and burn with a chef's blowtorch.

Best served with fresh berries, orange segments and fruit biscotti (see recipe on page 144).

Cranberry biscotti

INGREDIENTS

125g caster sugar

125g plain flour

1 and a half tsp baking powder

50g dried cranberries

50g raisins

2 medium eggs

METHOD

Pre-heat the oven to 160 degrees centigrade.

Mix all the dry ingredients (everything except the eggs) together.

Beat the eggs and add them to the dry mix.

Pour the mix onto a baking tray in lines approximately 4cm wide, with a 5cm gap in between them.

Cook for 30 minutes, then take out of the oven and leave to cool.

Turn the oven down to 90 degrees centigrade. Once the biscotti have cooled, cut into portions approximately 1 centimetre each.

Put the biscotti back in to the oven at 90 degrees centigrade until dry (approximately 20 minutes).

Banana parfait

IN A CHOCOLATE SHELL WITH RAISIN PURÉE, LIME ICE CREAM AND LIME DUST

INGREDIENTS

For the banana parfait:

2 very ripe bananas (put in freezer the night before)

300g dark chocolate (for the shell)

280ml double cream

Half leaf gelatine, plus cold water to soak it in

1 egg

3 egg yolks

15ml glucose

50g caster sugar

100g caramel, broken into small pieces

You will also need:

Acetate sheets

Metal cooking rings, 5cm (2in) deep

An ice cream machine

METHOD

Peel the frozen bananas and purée them in a blender. Cut 8 pieces of acetate into bands to fit inside your metal rings, ensuring they have an overlap.

In the restaurant we temper chocolate to give it a shine and a crisp finish. This is a technical skill that you can look up on the internet, but if you cannot do it, it's not a problem. Just melt your chocolate in a heatproof bowl over a pan of boiling water, or a bain-marie if you have one, until melted. If you have a thermometer, make sure the chocolate does not exceed 40 degrees centigrade. Next, spread the chocolate onto the acetate bands and carefully place in your rings with the spread side facing inwards. Allow to set in a cool place.

Whisk the 280ml of double cream until it forms soft peaks and leave aside for a moment. Soak the gelatine in cold water, enough to cover.

Whisk the one whole egg, three egg yolks, glucose and caster sugar together in a heatproof bowl over a pan of boiling water, or a bain-marie if you have one, until thick – this should take about 5 minutes. Add the puréed banana and soaked gelatine, then continue whisking off the heat until cooled to room temperature. Fold in the whipped cream and the caramel pieces, then carefully spoon into the moulds lined with chocolate. Freeze until firm.

Continued on the next page...

Banana parfait

INGREDIENTS

For the lime ice cream:
250ml milk
250ml cream
3 egg yolks
100g white sugar
Zest and juice of 3 limes

For the raisin purée:
100g raisins
100ml water
20g white sugar

For the lime dust:
Zest of 3 limes

METHOD

Bring the milk and cream to the boil in a saucepan and remove from the heat. Whisk the egg yolks and sugar together and add to the cream mix. Stir on the heat until thick, bring off the heat and add the lime juice and zest to the mix. Put into a cold container and cool down. In the restaurant we put this ice cream base into a Pacojet tin, leave to freeze and use the machine the next day to churn 20 portions out. At home you can use an ice cream machine to do this.

Put the raisins, water and sugar into a pan and bring to the boil. When the raisins are soft (after about 5 minutes), put into a blender and blitz the mix. Once blitzed, put it through a sieve to make it nice and smooth. Cool the mix down before serving.

Get the zest from the limes and put into an oven on a baking tray at a temperature of about 60 degrees centigrade. Once the zest has dried with no added colour, blitz it up in a blender and you have the lime dust.

TO SERVE

De-mould the parfaits by carefully removing the acetate. Serve with the raisin purée pulled across the plate, a quenelle of the lime ice cream (made into an oval or egg shape using two spoons) and a little dust scattered around the plate.

Rich dark chocolate fondant

WITH ICE CREAM AND WHITE CHOCOLATE SAUCE

Serves 10

INGREDIENTS

350g dark chocolate

300g butter, plus 10g softened butter for greasing

9 eggs

9 egg yolks

200g caster sugar

8 tbsp plain flour

2 tbsp 70% dark chocolate powder

You will also need:

10 ramekins or fondant moulds

METHOD

Pre-heat the oven to 180 degrees centigrade.

Melt the butter and chocolate together in a heatproof bowl over a pan of boiling water, or a bain-marie if you have one.

Whilst the chocolate is melting, whisk the eggs, egg yolks and sugar together until it is light and has tripled in size.

Stir the flour into the melted butter and chocolate.

Fold the chocolate into the egg mixture.

Grease the fondant moulds using the softened butter, and sprinkle on the dark chocolate powder.

Pour the fondant mix into the moulds, leaving approximately 2cm from the top.

Refrigerate until completely solid – at least 1 hour.

Cook in the oven for 8 minutes. The fondants are cooked when they have risen, and when you press the top you can feel the centre has turned liquid but the outside retains its shape. Leave to stand for 2 minutes before serving.

Best served with fresh strawberries, white chocolate sauce (see opposite) and caramel ice cream. Use additional fruit for garnish if preferred, as shown in picture overleaf.

Plain ice cream base

INGREDIENTS

500ml double cream

3 egg yolks

70g caster sugar

METHOD

Bring the cream up to the boil.

Whisk the egg yolks together with the sugar.

Pour the boiling cream onto the eggs and sugar mix.

Whisk to combine.

Leave to cool, then place the mixture into a freezer until set.

Add your own flavours, such as caramel or chocolate, to this base as desired.

White chocolate sauce

INGREDIENTS

100g white chocolate

100ml double cream

METHOD

Heat the cream in a saucepan until boiling, then take off the heat.

Add the chocolate to the cream and stir until the chocolate is completely dissolved.

Rich dark chocolate fondant with ice cream and white chocolate sauce

Lemon & ginger cheesecake

Serves 8-12

Chef's tip: Use the 15 egg whites you have left over to make a meringue.

INGREDIENTS

750g ginger biscuits

175g melted butter

12 gelatine leaves, plus water to soak them in

15 egg yolks

250g caster sugar

2 vanilla pods

Juice of 3 lemons

500g full fat cream cheese

1 litre double cream

You will also need:

20cm square cake tin

METHOD

Crush the biscuits and add the melted butter. Meanwhile, soak the gelatine leaves in cold water.

Press the crushed biscuit and butter mix evenly into the cake tin and refrigerate.

Put the egg yolks and sugar into a mixing bowl and whisk until the mixture is light and has tripled in size. Put to one side.

Deseed the vanilla pods and put the seeds into a mixing bowl with the lemon juice, cream cheese and cream. Mix until whipped into soft peaks.

Melt the gelatine leaves in a pan with a very small amount of water, then add to the cream mix.

Fold the egg mix and cream together, pour onto the biscuit base and leave to set in the fridge for 4 hours.

Best served with raspberry sorbet (see recipe on page 149) and berry coulis.

Raspberry sorbet

Makes 15 portions

INGREDIENTS

250ml water

175g granulated sugar

Juice of half a lemon

450g shop-bought raspberry coulis

METHOD

Bring the water and sugar up to boil to turn it into a light syrup. If necessary, stir to ensure the sugar is dissolved.

Take off the heat and add the lemon juice and raspberry coulis.

Allow to cool, then put into a freezer and take out every 1-2 hours to break up the ice crystals with a fork. After around 4 hours, it should be ready.

Buttermilk pannacotta

WITH RASPBERRY JELLY
AND CHANTILLY CREAM

Serves 8

INGREDIENTS

For the pannacotta:

7 gelatine leaves, plus cold water to soak them in

100g caster sugar

750ml cream

1 vanilla pod

750ml buttermilk

You will also need:

8 serving bowls, 1.5cm deep

For the raspberry jelly:

3 gelatine leaves

100ml water, plus some cold water to soak the gelatine leaves in

300ml raspberry coulis

For the Chantilly cream:

300ml double cream

1 vanilla pod

50g icing sugar

METHOD

Soak the gelatine leaves in cold water until soft.

Put the sugar and cream into a saucepan. Split the vanilla pod in half, scrape out the seeds and add these to the pan as well. Bring this to the boil, then take off the heat and stir in the soaked gelatine leaves.

Pass the buttermilk through a sieve into the mixture, mix thoroughly and pour into the serving bowls.

Leave in the fridge to set for 2 hours.

Once the pannacotta has set in the base of the bowl, garnish the top with with fresh strawberries, raspberry jelly (see below), crushed meringue, Chantilly cream (see below) and berry coulis.

Soak the gelatine leaves in cold water.

Add the 100ml of water to the coulis and bring to boil.

Add the soaked gelatine leaves to the coulis, stir until dissolved then pass though a fine sieve.

Allow to cool, then put in the fridge to set – a minimum of 4 hours, or preferably overnight.

Deseed the vanilla pod.

Put the vanilla seeds, the cream and the icing sugar into a bowl and whip with a balloon whisk until you create soft peaks.

Cheese

A selection of regular cheeses served in Cocina Restaurant

Smoked Applewood Cheddar

Softer and creamier than most cheddars, Smoked Applewood is a semi-hard cheese with a yummy smoky, tangy flavour. It's dusted with paprika which enhances the smokiness, adds a touch of sweetness and gives the cheese a wonderful golden glow.

Smoked Applewood Cheddar

Mahón Cheese

Also known as 'Minorcan' cheese, this fresh cheese is made on the Balearic Islands with raw or pasteurised cow's milk from the Fresian, Mahonesa or Minorcan and/or Alpine Brown breeds. Small amounts (no more than five per cent) of sheep's milk from the Minorcan breed are also allowed. It is rectangular, with rounded edges and a cleft on the top left by the knot of the cloth (the 'fogasser') used as a mould. The cheese is medium to large, very tall, and weighs up to 5 kilos or more. The rind is smooth and closed, and its colour varies between ivory white and intense yellow. It has a characteristic flavour, slightly acidic, salty and a bit buttery. Depending on its ageing, it can be milky and moist when it is fresh, or dry, sharp and somewhat spicy as the ageing time is lengthened.

Manchego

Manchego cheese is the most important and well-known sheep's milk cheese in Spain. The shape of this cheese is very characteristic and defined, due to the traditional use of esparto grass moulds which imprint a zigzag pattern along the side of the cheese. The small wooden boards used for pressing the cheese also imprint the characteristic wheat ear pattern.

Manchego

**Tuxford and
Tebbutt Stilton**

Brie de Meaux

Tuxford and Tebbutt Stilton

Stilton is called 'the King of English cheeses'. Our Blue Stilton is characterised by its typical blue veining with rich complex flavours and a piquant finish.

Mrs Kirkham's Lancashire

With Mrs Kirkham's Lancashire, the texture is as important as the flavour, and both are great. The flavour is a deep, mouth-filling mixture of citrus, lemony acidity with buttery, savoury richness. The texture is a moist, buttery, breadcrumb-like crumble which somehow opens the flavour up. This is a traditional Lancashire cheese made by the Kirkham family at Lower Beesley Farm in Goosnargh, Lancashire. They use small quantities of liquid starter cultures, allowing the cheese to develop acidity slowly which in turn allows other savoury, creamy, rich flavours to develop too. The distinctive thing about this Lancashire is that each cheese is made from a combination of curd from two different days. This is done to taste, altering the quantities to balance out the acidity, as the older curd will have stronger acidity. The cheese is then bound in buttered muslin, which allows some moisture to escape during maturation, and kept for four months.

Brie de Meaux

Brie de Meaux has the sweetness one would expect from a top world cheese. It delivers a very soft combination of hazelnut and fruit aromas.

PEPERONCINO
19'90
P.V.P. € QUILO

Index

Continued on the next page...

Mushrooms

Field mushroom linguine with red pepper and chilli, *90*
Grilled Portobello mushroom, sun-blushed tomato, buffalo mozzarella and rocket in toasted sourdough, *136*

Orange

Burnt Catalan cream, *142*

Pannacotta

Buttermilk pannacotta with raspberry jelly and Chantilly cream, *154*

Pasta

Field mushroom linguine with red pepper and chilli, *90*
Penne pasta with chorizo and smoked bacon in a spicy tomato sauce, *93*

Peas

Saddle of Walton Lodge new season lamb with broad beans, peas and a redcurrant and rosemary jus, *104*

Peppers

Chargrilled vegetable salad, *78*
Field mushroom linguine with red pepper and chilli, *90*
Pimientos de Padrón, *122*

Pork

Albondigas con tomate, *113*
Chilli and lavender scented Walton Lodge pork belly with a root vegetable sauerkraut, potato fondant and a red wine and apple sauce, *99*
Paella, *32*

Potato

Chargrilled tuna niçoise, *81*
Chilli and lavender scented Walton Lodge pork belly with a root vegetable sauerkraut, potato fondant and a red wine and apple sauce, *99*
Hake, cheese and chive croquettes, *118*
Oven roast chicken supreme with mashed potato, truffled baby leeks, pancetta bacon and baby gem, *61*
Pan-seared fillet of brill with a warm new potato, fennel and green bean salad and sauce vierge, *70*
Roast duck with a celeriac purée, grilled asparagus, roasted new potatoes and a red wine and cherry jus, *108*

Prawns

Gambas pil pil, *116*
Paella, *32*

Raspberry

Buttermilk pannacotta with raspberry jelly and Chantilly cream, *154*
Raspberry sorbet, *153*

Rice

Paella, *32*
Roasted monkfish wrapped in serrano ham with a crab, lemon and chilli risotto, *68*

Salad

Chargrilled tuna niçoise, *81*
Chargrilled vegetable salad, *78*
Chicken Caesar salad, *82*

Sandwiches

Barça pepito (steak sandwich), *135*
Casa club sandwich, *139*
Grilled Portobello mushroom, sun-blushed tomato, buffalo mozzarella and rocket in toasted sourdough, *136*

Squid

Cajun calamari, *114*
Paella, *32*

Tomato

Albondigas con tomate, *113*
Barça pepito (steak sandwich), *135*
Casa club sandwich, *139*
Chargrilled tuna niçoise, *81*
Chargrilled vegetable salad, *78*
Grilled Portobello mushroom, sun-blushed tomato, buffalo mozzarella and rocket in toasted sourdough, *136*
Pan con tomate, *121*
Penne pasta with chorizo and smoked bacon in a spicy tomato sauce, *93*

Written by:
Steve Perez
with Adam Kay

Contributors:
Andy Wilson, John Brailsford, David Prince, John Hattersley, Javier De La Hormaza

Edited by:
Paul Orton

Design by:
Richard Abbey

Photography by:
© Jodi Hinds Photography
www.jodihinds.com
Additional photographs supplied by Casa Hotel

First published in 2014 on behalf of:
Casa Hotel – www.casahotels.co.uk
Lockoford Lane, Chesterfield, S41 7JB
Tel: 01246 245 999

Published by:
RMC Books – www.rmcbooks.co.uk
6 Broadfield Court, Sheffield, S8 0XF
Tel: 0114 250 6300